A MAN OF RESPECT

It has never happened before. Until now we had heard of *pentiti*, those who repented: repentant terrorists and *mafiosi*, whose declared aim was to cleanse their souls and whose real motive was to engineer a good slice of remission. But Giovanni, the protagonist of this extraordinary chronicle of a life wholly spent on 'the wrong side', repents nothing and makes no attempt at self-justification. Nor is he pleading for the mercy of a court. There is, in fact, no threat of court proceedings hanging over his head. He is not only anonymous to the reader, but also to the law.

Giovanni's life spans the history of the modern Mafia which, having vegetated for decades in the Sicilian farmlands, grubbing for a pittance and tolerating mediaeval paternalism, woke up with a start after the war and within a few years had graduated to high quality crop cultivation, then to smuggling cigarettes and then, via the get-rich-quick mania of the building rackets, to heroin. The income is no longer a pittance, and no trace of tolerance remains. It is easy enough to pass judgement on all this, less easy to do so reading Giovanni's story, in which murder in cold blood is tempered constantly with a tenacious sense of honour and an almost manic determination to be respected. This makes it difficult to decide whether thought and action are simply the result of 'professional' training, or the inevitable consequence of a childhood and adolescence spent in poverty and ignorance, or if they derive from an inexorable genetic code, as ancient as the island itself.

'There are truth the author tells us in his br Giovanni's tale is told as his means that even the d rial worth pondering. Fro the trial in Palermo, from or 'crimes of honour', all n a stance that may arouse indignation, but may also raise doubts in our minds. One – the most grave – above all. A state that abrogates its responsibilities may thrust its adults into violence in the same way that a family that abrogates its responsibilities thrusts its adolescents into drugs and self-destruction.

A MAN OF RESPECT

The True Story of a Mafia Assassin

Anonymous
Translated from the Italian by
Avril Bardoni

A Pan original
Pan Books   London, Sydney and Auckland

First published in Great Britain 1991 by
Pan Books Ltd, Cavaye Place, London SW10 9PG

1 3 5 7 9 8 6 4 2

ISBN 0 330 30704 5

Printed in England by Clays Ltd, St Ives plc

Foreword

Like every Sicilian of average culture who keeps himself reasonably well informed, I thought I knew everything there was to know about the Mafia. Like everyone else, I followed Tommaso Buscetta's trial and the verbose confessions which resulted in prison sentences totalling 2,665 years for his former colleagues.

But the Mafia as reported by Buscetta inhabits a rarefied and lofty region; it is remote and shadowy. The other Mafia, the ordinary Mafia that no one knows, was described to me in a series of interviews that took place surrounded by a secrecy both theatrical and genuinely dramatic, by a man whose 'Family' had been completely wiped out by the Corleonesi and their associates who, in the space of a few years, accomplished a feat never before attempted and imposed a *pax romana* upon the island. In Palermo today, the guns only 'sing' for zealous servants of the state, infiltrators, police informers and those associates who have outlived their usefulness.

This account, of completely uncontrived value as an historical document, slowly traces the evolution of the *piovra* (the deliberate, systematic ruining of a person or an enterprise) from the time-honoured practice confined to the post-Bourbon feudal lands, through the semi-urbanized protection rackets associated with market gardens, the *giardini*, and then the violent roughhouse of the illegal building industry, to what may prove to be its definitive form, tied in with politics and intoxicated with the profits of the drug trade.

The narrator is always the same man; we see him first as a boy, too young to understand what is happening around him and to him, naïvely enthusiastic about an ideology based upon personal respect rather than money, acknowledging the authority of prestige rather than the gun, and bound by unwritten rules as absolute as divine decrees. As he matures he becomes more cynical, but also shrewder. The world in which he grew up has changed, leaving him with a scarred body and alone.

This is the story told in the book: it is history seen from below, an autobiographical journey from involvement with the godfathers of the land to those of the heroin market; it is a confession with no repentance, no regrets. I noted it down and transcribed it without ever straying from the facts, interpreting the language to the best of my ability. I have probably dwelt at greater length than he would approve upon the first years of my subject's life, on the mafioso 'imprinting' he underwent, and the subsequent development of personality and behaviour.

It was inevitable that an ambiguous emotional empathy should eventually develop between subject and writer. To begin with, I tried to camouflage this because it made me feel uneasy and because I was afraid that my patience and eagerness to understand would be mistaken for ideological complicity. Then I stopped worrying about it. If the book inspires moralistic debate rather than the usual reviews, so be it: that will not conceal the great lesson of life from those who have ears to hear it: namely, that there are truths in hell and lies in Paradise.

The author

I

You can't see the sea from my village. They built it on top
of a mountain like they always used to do in olden times,
but there are other mountains all around it. In summer
it's too hot and in winter too cold. New roads have now
put the nearest coastal city within a half-hour's drive, but
when I was a child it meant six hours by donkey-cart or
two hours by the *postale*, and I was fifteen before I had
my first glimpse of it.

My uncle Bartolo was a carter and knew all the
villages in the province. He was quite a character and
always cheerful. He loved to talk about all the things
he saw as he travelled around, and he did so with the
skill of a troubadour, inventing freely whenever the need
arose. My father called him *sceccu allegru*[1] because he
had no land, no home, no family and no responsibilities.
My mother, his sister, said he had always been a half-wit.
But when he came to see us and started to tell his stories,
they both hung on his every word and ended up by laughing just as much as we children did.

Uncle Bartolo – *Zu Vàrtulu* in dialect – had often
talked about the sea and I had gathered that it must
be extremely big; but I had also realized his capacity for
talking bullshit and making it sound like Gospel truth, so
I was not altogether convinced. When we got there after
a whole morning in the donkey cart under a blazing sun,
I was so tired that I had fallen asleep. As we reached the
top of a hill, Zu Vàrtulu rapped me on the head with the
handle of his whip.

'Look, there it is!'

I couldn't utter a word before we got to the beach: I felt lost. He was chatting away and joking, but I was tongue-tied. Then he told me to stay where I was and not to take it into my head to bathe. I was to wait there while he attended to some business.

It was towards the end of May and lunchtime, so there was hardly anybody in sight. I sat down on the sand but retreated rapidly when the water started coming towards me. Then I realized that there was no danger because after a moment it went away again. But I was still bewildered and more than a little anxious.

After a while two older boys came past; they were wearing short trousers and their legs were dark brown. I watched them to see if they were looking at me. They, I thought, must know all about the sea, and there were a thousand questions I should have liked to ask. But I was afraid they would think me ignorant. My father was fond of saying that the wisest words were those left unsaid. I have never forgotten that.

When my uncle returned, I ran to him with my arms outspread like Christ on the cross, as if to say: This is unbelievable! And he laughed, as pleased and gratified as if the sea were something he had made himself. He asked me what I thought of it all, and I said that the most astonishing thing was that the water instead of running parallel to its banks as it usually did, ran *up* to the beach, and kept coming higher and higher, yet without ever overflowing. This made him laugh more than ever. '*Testa vacanti*!',[2] he said.

The road home was nearly all uphill. As it was getting late and I was tired out, Zu Vàrtulu thought I would go to sleep at once. But I was still feverishly excited and kept asking him questions about the sea, the fish, the storms; and as there were some things even he didn't know about, he eventually got cross, gave me another rap on the head with the handle of the whip and told me to go to sleep.

I was the youngest of five. My father hired himself out by the week, but we also had two *tumoli*[3] of arable land. All the plots were the same in those days: maize and almonds – some strips of fruit and vegetables where the good Lord had provided water. There was no house in the fields, only a reed hut where my father, my two brothers and I slept during the weeks of hoeing, planting and harvesting. It was a masculine existence, with no women to wash or cook for us. Midday and evening we ate bread with olives and onions washed down, for me too, by a mouthful of wine.

Out in the fields my father was a different person. At home he rarely spoke to us: he never laughed and didn't like any chattering. We all ate from a communal platter, using tin spoons to scoop up the pasta – always the short-cut kind – and a sauce of tomatoes or peas or beans, whichever happened to be in season. But when we were working in the fields we lit a fire in the evening and sat around it roasting black olives, and my father would tell us what it used to be like in his boyhood, about his father and about his grandfather who had once seen Don Peppino Garibaldi close to. And he was always jolly, chatting and joking with all three of us, even with me, the youngest.

Then the family scattered to the winds. One evening my eldest brother, Borino, announced that he was going to Argentina. It was a time of partings: whole families were disappearing. People were saying that there was work and land available in Argentina for anyone who wanted it. My father warned him that if he once left home he'd better not show his face again. My mother wept secretly and said nothing. Then one Sunday there

3

was a knock on the door; it was the agent collecting up the emigrants, and Borino went. As he couldn't write, he never sent a letter and we never knew what became of him.

My sister Assuntina died of meningitis as a small child and I don't remember anything about her. My other sister, Gina, married a local man who went to work in Grugliasco, near Turin. As she was sixteen and I was seven when she left, and as we didn't see each other for ten years, we were never close. I once went to visit her, but my brother-in-law is an ignorant sonofabitch who thinks he's no end of a fine fellow just because he lives in the north. So, not wanting to create problems for my sister, I have never visited her again, but every now and then I send a little present for her or the girls, even though neither of them was called after our mother.

My other brother was a really good lad. His name was Totò. He, too, went away to work, to Belgium. He was a miner; hard work but very well paid. We got letters from Totò, some written by himself, others by friends. He used to send a bit of money and every summer, without fail, he would come home for two weeks, bringing everyone presents that my mother put away in the linen-chest under her bed. It was lucky that when Totò died in a mining accident I was already earning and could help out at home, because by that time my father was too old and too ill to work and the two *tumoli* alone couldn't provide all the necessities of life.

My father had been working as a day-labourer ever since the Cavaliere, who had given him work for thirty years, sold all his land without any warning. Since leaving school I had been going off to work with him. I had had three years of elementary school, always with the same teacher, who taught us in a long, narrow room above the kitchen of her own home. When her father – a little old man with a white moustache who was as thin as a rake – came home around midday, the teacher would set us some work to be getting on with and go down to the kitchen to fry *polpette*. Who could possibly think about lessons with that heavenly smell drifting upstairs? So when she got back she laid into us with the cane while her father chuckled and coughed.

At the end of the third year she met my father one evening and told him that she had no choice but to fail me because, although I was bright, I didn't work at my books. It was common knowledge that the teacher could be bribed, by a lamb at Easter or a slice of fresh ginger-bread every now and then, to wink at the odd failure or provide a bit of coaching, but where my family was concerned it was already a luxury for me to be at school instead of working, and there was no Easter lamb, even for ourselves.

As soon as I got home my father said, 'We'll be leaving at four o'clock tomorrow morning. He's coming with me to the farm.' My mother said nothing and I was quite content to go with him. I wasn't yet old enough to understand much about life, but I was already of the opinion that school was not for the likes of us.

I had never been to Piano di Maggio, but my father had spoken about it for years and I felt as if I had been born there. It was an extremely large farm, with many buildings and very few windows, as was usual in those days. It took two hours to get there on the back of a mule; the road was deserted and there were no farmhouses to be seen because the land here was poor and sandy and nearly all of it was owned by the government.

Piano di Maggio belonged to the Cavaliere, a hand-some man, tall and straight-backed. He owned a Fiat car. The first time he saw me he asked my father to tell him my name and gave me ten lira as a present. That was forty years ago and I can still remember the feel of the banknote in my hand.

After the first few weeks, the farm manager noticed that I was coping well and that I would run to draw water for the men when they needed it without having to be asked. So every Saturday he would add something for me to my father's pay-packet. I don't know how much this was, but I heard my father say to my mother: 'Giovannino's beginning to earn his living.'

At night we slept in a kind of storeroom; it was long and high and had bars at the windows. Between twenty and thirty men slept on sacks of straw laid on the floor. At harvest time, and when the olives were being picked, there could be as many as fifty. It was fine in the winter, but too hot in the summer, so I used to slip out secretly and sleep under a fig tree near the Cavaliere's house.

At home there was no way of escaping from the heat of midsummer. The most my father could do was to leave the door half open at night, because the house had no windows and there was not enough air for everybody. My mother objected to this because the house was on ground level and sometimes a hungry dog or a rat wandered in. But in the winter, while my parents, my brothers and sisters snuggled up in pairs, I, who was the odd one out and the smallest, went to sleep in the manger and it was the mule who kept me warm. Every now and then she would nibble me, but not out of viciousness: she was probably trying to snatch a mouthful of hay and couldn't see very well in the dark.

The Cavaliere was nothing like the landowners I knew in the village. He was a city gentleman, always elegantly dressed. Not even Baron Valente, who I saw coming out of church every Sunday, wore a white suit. When he visited the stables he always stopped outside the door. His wife never came to Piano di Maggio, but this didn't worry him because the farm manager's wife and the mother of one of the *campieri*[4] looked after the house. There were nearly always guests coming for supper and staying the night, friends who came from Palermo or even from Rome and said '*Bello!*' or '*Bellissimo!*' at everything they saw, including the hens. They apparently didn't have hens where they came from.

They ate chicken and sausages roasted over the fire, with artichokes when these were in season. But the chickens were always cooked in some fancy way, and after the meal the Cavaliere put aside a plate for my father and the farm manager with the skin, the heads and any bones that still had a little meat on them. I was crazy about the heads.

Although my father was not permanently employed like the farm manager and the *campieri*, the Cavaliere found work for him throughout the summer and in the winter, too, whenever possible. I cannot honestly say that we lacked for anything. The only problems concerned the house. Even after all these years I am haunted by the memory of the annual upheaval on 31 August. In those days, 31 August was the day when all the tenancy agreements for the year expired and the new ones came into force. Things have changed now, what with the introduction of the fair rent system and a whole lot of other reforms, but then it was quite simple: the outgoing tenant loaded everything on to a cart on the thirty-first, and if he didn't have a cart of his own he borrowed one.

No one in the village slept that night. Those who arrived early had to wait for the others to move out, and if the ones who were leaving were late clearing the house, the new tenants piled all their belongings outside the door and waited to take possession. There were heated quarrels that stirred up whole neighbourhoods.

My father, however, was a man of peace, always punctual when it came to quitting the house and always ready to help the people whose house he was taking over.

My brother Borino was more fond of me than of anyone else in the family. Before he went off to Argentina, we sometimes used to go to work together. Not that often, because my father always wanted my help, even though he was the only one who got paid, but I was always delighted when it happened. Borino never hit me – apart from the occasional kick in the pants to tell me to get a move on – but he joked with me and treated me like an equal. Occasionally, when he rolled his cigarette with strong tobacco and crinkly paper, he even let me light it for him.

One evening on the Feast of the Immaculate Conception, he took me to the only prostitute in the village, who was called Mariannina. She was as wide as a church door, but had skin as white as snow and wore make-up and perfume. People said that she was over fifty, but I vaguely remember her as a fine-looking woman. This visit on the Feast of the Immaculate Conception was an old tradition in the village, and there was a crowd outside her door. I was in a fever of excitement, but when our turn came, Mariannina took a good close look at me and then turned to my brother.

'How old is he?'

'Old enough,' replied Borino, wise in the ways of the world. And he caressed her face. But caresses got him nowhere: she was scared. The *maresciallo*[5] had been very clear on this point: no minors.

'But how will the *maresciallo* ever know unless you tell him yourself?' asked my brother. Mariannina laughed. She went to the window and drew the curtain back a fraction. There must have been about fifteen men standing outside, smoking and chatting as they waited their turn.

'Never mind,' said Borino consolingly as we went home. 'Wait until one comes along from outside the village, when the fair's here. The others are all better than Mariannina.'

But another chance never came. Borino was out of work all winter. It was a lean time: there was no work even in building or herding goats. And then tragedy struck: the mule died one night without even a whimper. And because some ill-wisher poked his nose into the business, a health inspector arrived on the trot and said we couldn't sell the animal to the butcher because no one knew what she'd died of and there could be some infection.

So what with one thing and another, when the spring came Borino left for good. Two years later Totò went too, but Borino had always been my real big brother, the one who had made everyone else respect me. Don't get me wrong: I was quite capable of standing up for myself, but the older boys, who had kept their distance when Borino was around, now began to give me a hard time. I defended myself, but always came off worst, and when I got home there was more trouble, because my father was not the type to rush out brandishing a hoe and threatening the other boy's father just because his son had come home with a bloody nose.

He, who was too much of a gentleman and indeed would die for being too much of a gentleman, always blamed me for starting the fights, saying that I caused them because I was out of work and was naturally quarrelsome. I was, he said, a *cani 'rraggiatu*.[6] So he sent me to work for a market-gardener, no pay, just a bag of vegetables every now and then. I enjoyed hoeing the rows because it meant standing with my feet in the water, but the man himself was a nasty piece of work. He gave me very little to eat, and if I made a mistake I got a taste of the whip. But when he wanted to give me a taste of something else I left. My father beat me for it because I was too shy to tell him the real reason and he assumed I didn't want to work.

Meanwhile, Zu Vàrtulu hadn't deserted us; he actually dropped in quite often, but after Borino went away things were never quite the same again. He never stayed long: just said hello and goodbye. And realizing that there was never half a lira in the house, he would slip his sister a bit on the quiet. I know because I saw him do it once.

My mother was very cunning when it came to spending those few lira. She always bought things that she already had in the house like oil, corn and beans. So my father never noticed anything but was happy to see how long the supplies were lasting. Occasionally, she would also buy a cheap dress or a pair of American shoes for my sister Gina and, during the *fiera*, bits and bobs that men don't see because they don't concern them. Once my father noticed that we had a new frying pan, but my mother explained that she had got it in exchange for a few beans, which was how one did things in those days.

One winter's evening, Zu Vàrtulu arrived with a basket of sorb-apples and half a round of pecorino cheese. He always brought something with him when he came to eat and sleep with us because he didn't want to be a burden. When Borino was still at home, and before my sister Assuntina died, he had always slept in the storeroom, but there was plenty of space in the main room now and my mother was always happy when her brother spent the night with us. That evening, as I was trying to get to sleep, I heard my uncle ask my father:

'And Giovannino, what's he up to these days?'

'Not much. When there's work to be done I take him along with me. The rest of time he just knocks about the streets.'

'Then I'll take him off with me for a few days.'

End of conversation. My uncle was the sort of man who knew how to get his own way. When he had decided about something and wanted no argument about it, he acted as if there was nothing to argue about. My father simply shrugged his shoulders. There was nothing in the world that could ruffle him once he'd had a glass of wine.

'*U Signuri v'accumpagna*,'[7] he said, adding that he wasn't to keep me away long because as soon as the rain stopped we had to go collecting firewood in the fields. They went to sleep; but I lay there with eyes as round as saucers. I had never been away with my uncle for more than a day and my heart was thumping with excitement. I curled up under the blanket in the dark, thinking: 'Tomorrow we're off!'

Little did I imagine that a whole new life was about to start.

Notes

1. Happy-go-lucky.
2. Empty head.
3. *Tumolo*: a Sicilian land measurement equivalent to 2143 sq.m. or roughly half (0.529) an acre.
4. *Campieri*: field guards or supervisors, a Sicilian institution frequently open to abuse by the Mafia.
5. *Maresciallo*: Marshal, an officer of the *carabinieri* of an equivalent rank to Inspector. Note: the Italian Police Force is a branch of the armed services and all terminology relating to it, including ranks, is military.
6. Rabid dog.
7. 'May the Lord be with you.'

II

Mussomeli was no different from my own village: the same barefoot children, chickens in wooden cages outside every door, streets infested with scrawny dogs. But we weren't there to sell pins and ladies' stockings. Zu Vàrtulu wanted to introduce me to a certain important person. So in the afternoon, when what he called 'the snake-time' (the hottest part of the day) was past, we made our way towards a farm near the village.

Four men were sitting under the shade of a trained vine in front of the house, straddling their chairs and resting their arms on the backs. They brightened when they saw my uncle and one of them, who had a drooping, narrow moustache, called out:

'Vàrtulu, what have you got for us this time, cocks' eggs?'

They all laughed. Farm-labourers who had been working nearby came up, and six or seven children and two fat women also appeared. Everyone seemed happy to see my uncle, who was chatting and joking in his own special way. And the more they laughed, the more he tried to make them laugh.

'Who's the young man, then, Vàrtulu?' asked the man with the moustache after a while. My uncle gave me a shove.

'Go and kiss his hand.'

Don Peppe Genco Russo[1] must have been about fifty-five at that time and no one would understand nowadays the aura surrounding such a man. I had already encountered a good few landowners, bosses and employers of other men's labour, and none of them did anything but give orders and watch their own interests. Nothing else mattered.

He was different. One could tell immediately that he was respected, not for what he had but for what he was, and respect is the most precious thing in life. Women, money and health come and go; but respect once lost has gone for ever. While I kissed the hand with its ring like a bishop's, I looked at his face and would have drunk it like a glass of fresh water because I liked it so much. He asked me what I did and what I wanted to be, and my uncle explained that there was no work for me in the village, but that I was able and keen to work and, above all, respectful.

'Surely on a farm like this some job could be found for a boy who only asks to be allowed to work!' cried Zu Vàrtulu, putting on a great act of desperation and burying his face in his hands. This time Don Peppe did not laugh.

'What makes you think we're short of *picciutteddi*[2] here at Mussomeli?' he said, and turned to me. 'So you reckon you're smarter than my *picciutteddi*, do you?'

'If you please, sir, yes I do,' I said, and was gratified to receive a slap from Don Peppe, who was laughing and winking at the other men.

'How's that for a smart answer, eh? Vàrtulu, your nephew certainly doesn't take after you: he's got a head on his shoulders. What's your name?'

'Giovannino.'

'Rosa, give Giovannino something to nibble.'

They gave me two hard, dry biscuits left over from Christmas. But on a day like that they could have given me stones and I would have said they were delicious. Nothing more happened on that occasion; I ate the

13

biscuits and barely said another word. But in the evening, at home, Zu Vàrtulu spun a tale about their wanting me to work with the cows and the calves and invented so much that I could hardly believe my ears. No names were mentioned. He just said they were people from the Mussomeli district and friends of his.

My father said nothing for or against the plan; my mother asked if the place was very far away and Zu Vàrtulu laughed.

'Far away? Compared to where his brothers have wound up, Giovannino's hardly going away at all; he'll be just around the corner . . . '

My father cut him short. 'We'll talk about it when the time comes,' he said.

The time didn't come for quite a while. I was seventeen before they sent for me, and heaven knows how many times Zu Vàrtulu had been there pleading with them. It was March. I thought I would be home again after the summer, but in the event I was away for more than thirty years. No such possibility occurred to my mother. She packed me a bag with enough bread for a week, plenty of cheese and even a little money, and gave me the same advice that all mothers give their sons.

But my father had a strange expression on his face, and murmured some words that I never forgot: '*E l'urtimi ascidduzzu si ni vulà.*'[3]

I was a stranger, an outsider in that place. This is an experience I was to suffer many times in my life. Every time it happened I thought of my brothers. Of Totò, God rest his soul, whose short life had been spent abroad, working underground, he who had been born under the open sky, beneath a tree. And Borino, who couldn't even speak Italian yet spent forty years of his life – if he is still alive – in a foreign country, surrounded by people speaking a foreign language.

I worked mainly with the calves, but every now and then I went out to pasture the cattle. Luckily, the Mussomeli cows and calves spoke the same language as cows and calves in my home village: the language of the stick. There was nothing hard or unpleasant about the work, but there were times when things happened that I, with my limited experience of life, found puzzling. I didn't stay in the same place all the time; sometimes I was sent to work on other farms for other people. And even the farm where my cows were was not the one Zu Vàrtulu had taken me to the day I met Don Peppe.

Although I was working, I was paid nothing the first year. Don Peppe had arranged for me to skip military service. 'You can learn to be a soldier here on the farm,' he used to say from time to time when he saw me. 'Do you agree?' But even though I wasn't being paid, I was fed and had somewhere to sleep and I was being taught a skill. Later they paid me, but not a regular weekly wage. I don't even know how much my daily pay was; the odd coin or two appeared from time to time and I said thank you and put it away because happily I did not really need money. As for food, there was enough and more than enough, and sometimes I would be given a pair of still serviceable trousers, a shirt and other necessary items. One day I hurt my foot and they took me to a doctor, and when he had finished putting in the stitches he grabbed hold of my ear and gave it a good tweak.

'Good lad. Didn't murmur while I was stitching him up.'

Once a month, and sometimes more often, there was a special day when Don Peppe hosted a party for important friends who came from other places; one could tell from the number-plates on their cars that some of them even came from Palermo. We men did all the preparations, and the youngest had the job of providing the animals. The problem was not catching them, but finding a place where we could do what we had to without inconvenience to friends or influential visitors. We would work far away from the house, late in the evening, and then would be on our feet all night long, dealing with calves, pigs, sheep or whatever. We slaughtered them immediately and I disposed of the skins, burying them deep in the soil because otherwise the dogs would have smelt them and tried to dig them up.

The nice thing was that we all ate together. Three, four or five tables – according to the number of guests – would be prepared, and one of these was for us boys. Don Peppe laughed and joked with us, and there was meat for everyone, unlike the Piano di Maggio days when we were lucky to be given the chicken heads to gnaw.

I was always teased during these meals, not only because I was the youngest, but also because I came from another district and spoke a different dialect. This happens in Sicily: places only twenty kilometres apart have a different way of speaking and a different intonation of the voice. They would say 'Come on, Giovannino, let's hear how you speak.' If they were older than me I would smile and say nothing; if they were lads of my own age I would reply with the joke: 'What do you want me to say . . . ponce?' This amused even Don Peppe when he got to hear about it, and once he said: 'Go ahead, go ahead and tease him. When he's a bit older he'll give you all something to think about.'

I don't know how seriously he meant it, but he was right because I was already capable of making the others respect me once the joking was over. I feared no one. If one of them was bigger than me, I was quicker off the mark, and if he was quick off the mark, I was brighter.

One day, towards the end of April, I was out grazing the cows when I saw two shepherds approaching. They must have had about a hundred sheep with them, and when they got to the patch of grass the animals started to browse, inching forwards with their heads down. There was a one-eared dog with them, too, who went right up close to one of my cows, a brown cow called Bunuzza. Because she was frightened, she lowered her head and threatened him with her horns and the dog started barking and snapping at her heels; so I came up waving my stick and the dog made off pretty quickly.

'What do you think you're doing?' shouted the older of the two shepherds. He was probably around thirty and had the sly, brutish face of shepherds the world over.

I told him that my cows were already grazing on this patch and that he could take his sheep elsewhere. Hearing from my voice that I was from a different place, they both started laughing and pushing me about, asking if the cow I had defended was my mother and that other one my grandmother and another younger one my sister perhaps. They smashed my nose.

That evening I tried to hide away, but one of the lads saw me and told the farm manager who sent someone to fetch me immediately. The manager's still alive and has always been a decent fellow, so I won't mention his name. He was about forty, young in those days for someone in a position of responsibility, but he had a good head on his shoulders, was strong, reliable and a hard worker. He knew how to give orders even to men older than himself.

'Who was it?' he asked. He didn't even glance at my nose.

'Shepherds.'

'What shepherds?'

I remembered the dog with one ear, but the men's

17

faces were already a blank in my mind. He said nothing. I thought he probably didn't know them because men like that wander over large areas and sleep in a different place every night. Finally he shone a lamp on my face and had a good look at my nose.

'There's no infection there. Go to bed.'

By Sunday morning five days had passed and I had stopped thinking about it. Not that I'd forgotten about it: good or ill, I never forget anything done to me, but it was no longer preying on my mind and my nose wasn't even hurting any more. One of the boys had started to tease me in front of the others, saying he wanted to know how I spoke now that the shape of my nose had been changed. I had laid into him so ferociously that no one dared come between us.

At six o'clock the manager came to wake me. Mounted on a donkey, I followed him and his bay horse along roads and paths, some of which were familiar to me and others not. The ride lasted more than two hours and not a word was spoken. At last the road began to climb and on the right I saw a village that was not Mussomeli. There was a sheep-pen beside a house. Some people were making cheese and the one-eared dog came nosing around us inquisitively but without barking. There were four shepherds, one an old man with white hair and the scar of an old knife-wound on his forehead.

'Hop down,' said the manager. The men were standing and looking hard at us. I had a knife in my pocket and was ready to use it, but there were four of them and they were all scowling. I couldn't understand why the manager hadn't brought his shotgun. He always carried a gun when he rode out on horseback.

'Do you recognize them?' he asked me. He was looking at me, not even glancing at the shepherds.

'Him and him,' I said. The manager went up to the

one who smashed my nose, and hit him across the face so hard that he fell to the ground. The old man said:

'The boys knew nothing. They didn't know he was your *picciutteddu*.'

'So they could have asked him who he was,' replied the manager. He had already turned his back on them and was remounting his horse. I was beside him. Even the one-eared dog had his tail between his legs.

Half an hour later, when we got to a place where the path was wide enough for us to ride abreast, he beckoned me.

'Now do you understand what respect means?'

'*Voscenza sì.*'[4]

Not once in two years had I ever seen him laugh, but he now turned to me with a grin that went from ear to ear.

'So from now on watch out, and if you ever allow people to walk all over you again, stay out of my sight!'

So far, however, I could still not claim to be a man. That moment arrived when I was nineteen, on the Feast of Corpus Christi in 1954, a year that was to be a turning-point in my life.

I was told to be prepared for something but I didn't know what. I had already been asked to do various small jobs from time to time, always with other people and never anything special. There are many ways of teaching a youngster. The best way is to make him afraid, and there is nothing easier. One evening I had heard Don Peppe tell an important friend of his: 'The biggest favour you can do a man is to teach him not to repeat a mistake.'

I noted this and put it into practice myself. I needed to learn all I could from such hints. Sometimes I learned about politics, matters concerning votes or trade unions, other times it was a matter of how to deal with bad behaviour, bad faith, debts that dragged on from day to day with promises but somehow never got paid. And in time I, too, learned my lesson: to keep my ears open and my mouth shut.

The farm manager explained what had to be done.

'A quick, efficient job is what's needed,' he told us. There were three of us.

In those days horses were our cars. When people in the countryside heard galloping hooves in the middle of the night, they would turn over in their beds and think of their sins, and in the morning they would go around with their eyes on the ground looking as if butter wouldn't melt in their mouths.

It was a small farm up in the mountains. There were three of us, led by a lad called Turidduzzu. He signalled to us to enter the stable while he placed himself, armed with a shotgun, in front of the house in case anyone should venture out while we were at work.

The moon was shining into the stall but even so you could hardly see a thing. The pig was in a corner while four scrawny heifers stood at the manger and about thirty sheep were at the far end, huddled together as sheep always are when they sleep, and the horns of a goat stuck up in the middle of the bunch.

'What's this, Noah's Ark?' said my companion. Being experienced at this sort of thing, he explained that we had to start with the pig.

'If he smells blood, all hell will be let loose. I'll deal with him.'

I had once seen a pig slaughtered. It had screamed like a human being and was still twitching even after the butcher had collected a pailful of blood. But this one was smaller and half asleep, apart from which my companion, who didn't have to worry about collecting the blood for a black pudding, stuck the knife straight into the heart instead of slitting the throat. The pig gave a squeal, but it was so soft that the other animals didn't even hear.

'Giovannino, don't waste any time, just one blow to the underbelly.'

I don't deny that I have done many nasty things in my time, and even if the people I've launched into eternity were no better than animals, they were still human; yet I have never felt such revulsion as I felt that night.

Some of the sheep raised their heads to see what I was doing to them, but others remained motionless even when I had done it. Either they fell silently, their forelegs buckled beneath them, or they uttered a feeble baa-aa with their tongues hanging out. Not one tried to escape.

It was worse with the cows. You can't imagine how much blood can come out of an animal that size. The straw was soaked as if it had been rained on for half an hour, and as the floor sloped, the blood ran down it and collected in a lake in the middle. I was used to walking through rain and mud and I don't mind if water gets into my shoes, but now, when I felt the wetness on my socks, I felt like cursing my mother for giving birth to me.

I heard my companion breathing heavily as if he had been running, and at every thrust of his knife he grunted like a pig. Every now and then a beast groaned or fell down with a thud; then all would be quiet again and the only sounds were those he was making and I realized that he, too, was worked up. In fact, he suddenly flew off the handle because the goat got away from him and he couldn't hold it still with only one hand grasping its horns.

'Vennecà, bagascia!'[5] he yelled, stabbing out blindly

all around him. I was thankful to be at the other end of the stable, or he might have struck me too. He was like a drunken man.

At that moment a rifle-shot rang out. In the silence of the surrounding countryside it sounded more like a cannon and dogs began to bark immediately in the distance. I couldn't tell whether it was just a warning shot or not, but I didn't care. I too was drunk with blood, I was swearing like a madman and would have gone on tirelessly working away with the knife even had there been a hundred or two hundred animals there.

'Come on!' shouted Turidduzzu, appearing in the doorway. At the same moment a woman in the house started to scream. She, too, sounded like an animal being slaughtered; it was eerie.

'Come on, Giovannino!'

I was alone in the stable now. The pile of sheep was still and the goat's horns no longer stuck up, but the cows were still alive, and when they heard me run towards the door, all four of them turned round to look at me. As I passed by, the one nearest to me stretched out her neck towards me, opened her mouth and vomited some more blood. The shouts continued from outside, and now a second woman had appeared.

'Giovannino!'

A second later I was on horseback, the knife still clutched in my hand.

Zu Vàrtulu was killed at the beginning of the summer. It happened at Aragona, a village in the province of Agrigento. 'A pedlars' brawl,' according to the *carabinieri*. I heard about it by chance and asked for leave of absence, but because my uncle was officially described as of no fixed abode and because I got there too late, they had already given him a pauper's burial without informing anyone. Not even my mother knew anything about it.

I went to the *caserma*[6] and spoke to the brigadier who came from Calabria. All I wanted was the name of the man who had killed my uncle, but I hadn't yet learned how policemen think. The way my uncle had died made the affair completely insignificant as far as they were concerned. After all the fuss about Turi Guiliano[7] a crime had to be major indeed before they took it seriously.

'A pedlars' brawl,' said the brigadier. 'The report states he died at the hands of person or persons unknown.'

'All I want to know is who did it.'

'I've already told you, son: person or persons unknown. Unknown means nobody knows who killed him. Men like him have no home and no family. They spend their lives going from one place to another . . . Who are you, anyway, a relative?'

He wanted to know my name, what I did, where I worked, how I had learned about the incident. He took more trouble finding out all about me than he did looking for the person or persons unknown, and when I told him as much his eyebrows shot up and he asked me whether I wanted to spend a night in the cells. But since it was nearly lunchtime, he let the matter drop. He refused to hand over Zu Vàrtulu's things, saying he would send them to the *carabinieri* in my village, and when I asked him how I could be sure he would do this, he yelled at me and threw me out.

It was already late in the evening when the Palermo *postale* put me down at the crossroads in Mussomeli. I

23

had eaten nothing all day but I wasn't hungry. I was thinking of that day on the beach in Gela when Zu Vàrtulu had given me my first sight of the most beautiful thing in the world. Even today, forty years later, I still remember it.

It rained on and off as I walked the fifteen kilometres to the farm. The next morning I was summoned to Don Peppe. Since the night of the Noah's Ark incident, when I had come through the test with flying colours, I had noticed that the other men now regarded me with more respect, and later something else happened that helped, too.

Again at night, a few of my mates and myself had been sent to the depot of a company that built roads. It was run by northern Italians, boneheads who couldn't or wouldn't ever learn. For this job we had a man from Riesi with us who knew how to handle explosives. I don't know how, but the police must have been tipped off and they were waiting for us inside. As soon as they fired the first shots over our heads I made a lightning decision and while the others ran off as fast as their legs would carry them, I climbed into the cabin of a steam roller.

Simple as that may sound, the fact is that no one thought of looking there because they had seen the others making for the fields. However, when the hullabaloo was over I saw people arriving from the village and the owners of the depot with them. I couldn't stay in the cabin, and had I tried to make a break for it they would have got me for sure. But I noticed some steel drums, the kind used for storing the water for mixing concrete, and I turned one upside down and crawled into it.

I wasn't afraid of the workmen finding me once the *carabinieri* had gone, but if they suspected nothing, so much the better because then the way home would be clear. Luckily, it wasn't summer, or the hot sun would have turned my steel overcoat into a coffin. But even so, after a whole day crouched inside it with neither food nor water, I was more dead than alive. But there are times when one has to endure certain things, and although I didn't yet know it, my capacity for endurance was to save my life on two or three occasions at least.

As soon as it was dark I made a run for it, steering well clear of roads and houses. When I reached the farm the following afternoon not even the dogs recognized me. The farm manager told me that I was the only one to return: all the others had been arrested and one was seriously wounded. Don Peppe was in Rome at the time, but he was back on Sunday and when he saw me he turned to the farm manager who was standing beside him and said:

'Remember what I said about this boy? I never make a mistake when it comes to judging character.'

As I was saying, the morning after my trip to Aragona Don Peppe sent for me. I knew that a man like him could have little time for a man like my uncle. But he kissed me and said how sorry he was. When I told him about my brush with the brigadier he said something that I have never forgotten.

'Even if you'd managed to find out the name of the culprit, you'd have had no right to do anything about it. I'm the one to tell you what to do and what not to do. We don't break bread together and then go off and break heads alone. Do you understand what I mean?'

'Voscenza sì.'

With his hand closed, he slipped a roll of banknotes, previously prepared, into my pocket.

'For the funeral expenses. Now go and break the news to your mother.'

Just like a father. How could I ever forget him?

Notes

1. *Giuseppe Genco Russo*. Born in 1894 and always overshadowed by the more powerful Calogero Vizzini, he controlled the area of Mussomeli, in the province of Caltanissetta. Unlike Vizzini, however, he had first-hand experience of the decline of his own generation; unknown to the flourishing new-style Mafia in Palermo, the Mafia of the *giardini* and the construction rackets, he was nevertheless a figure of considerable interest to the forces of justice who arrested, tried and imprisoned him in Lovere in the province of Bergamo. He was perhaps the first important member of the modern Mafia to be imprisoned.

2. *Picciutteddi*: Lads, but a diminutive of *picciotti*, a term frequently used for young mafiosi.

3. So the last chick has flown the nest.

4. A contraction of *vostra eccellenza*, this Sicilian expression is an extremely respectful form of 'Yes, sir.'

5. Come here, you bitch!

6. *Caserma*: barracks.

7. Salvatore Giuliano: the notorious bandit who terrorized this area of Sicily for seven years. He was finally caught and killed in 1950 at the age of twenty-seven.

III

I had the honour of being present at the funeral of
Don Calogero Vizzini.[1] I say honour because from all
those he could have chosen to accompany him from
Mussomeli, Don Peppe took only two lads, myself and a
certain Luciano, who eventually emigrated to America.
It was 1954 and the hottest July day I have ever known. I
wore a smart black suit, bought from a stall at the village
fiera because tailor-made clothes were beyond my reach.
Still, I was tall and broad-shouldered so the suit looked
as good as if it had been made for me and I knew that I
cut quite a dash in it.

Not that anybody, in that heat, gave us a second
glance. Luciano and I had to run from one end of
the village to the other checking everything that had
to be checked while we waited for Don Peppe and his
friends to arrive. There was to be an important meeting
before the funeral and they had arranged to hold it
in the house of a big landowner, one who carried
a great deal of weight in Villalba and who had been
a loyal friend of Don Calò's. Someone in his house
who knew everybody told me the names of the guests
as they arrived and I made mental notes because Don
Peppe wanted to be sure everyone was there before he
went in.

At the end of the meeting something happened which
took me quite by surprise. As Don Peppe passed by, arm
in arm with a man I knew only by sight, he saw me and
stopped.

'This is the *picciotto* I was telling you about. How does he strike you?'

The other man looked at me. He didn't have the presence of Don Peppe: he looked more like a farm manager, though you could tell that as a farm manager he would be a force to be reckoned with. He signalled his approval with a very slow, thoughtful nod.

'*Spertu pari*.[2] How old is he?'

'How old are you now, Giovannino? Twenty?' Don Peppe asked.

'*Voscenza no*. Nineteen.'

'Pay a visit to Riesi sometime, young man,' said the stranger, and he and Don Peppe walked on. Meanwhile, those following behind had heard everything, and as they passed me they looked at me with a certain interest. I stood there silently for a while, then turned to Luciano and with a jerk of my head asked him: 'Who was that?' Looking warily around him, he put his lips to my ear and whispered:

'Francesco Di Cristina.'[3]

In Riesi, the man I had taken for a farm manager ranked as high as Don Peppe in Mussomeli. I was puzzled at being shown such favour, I who was nothing but the dust beneath the feet of such men as these. I thought about it in church, during the service, and then throughout the night and the next few days. But at nineteen there was no way I could figure out something like this for myself.

In actual fact what had happened was this. My father's health kept getting worse and they were in a bad way at home. I had spoken to the farm manager about it, respectfully asking if I could do a job for myself, naturally well away from the village. He told me this was never, ever allowed and that was that. But one evening Don Peppe came out to the fields in great good spirits and at a certain point he took me by the arm and asked how things were going. I told him I needed money to send to my family, adding: 'I'd do anything for my mother and father.'

'There speaks a dutiful son,' he replied. Looking back, I can guess what he was thinking, that a desperate man can become a risk and it's best to get rid of him. But if the man is also a promising *picciotto*, then he may be able to do things that others wouldn't even attempt. This was why he had discussed me with Di Cristina: there was more action in Riesi, everyone said as much. There were plenty of big opportunities there, and I was looking for big opportunities. The kind of money I needed was just not to be had in Mussomeli, nor was there anything I could really get my teeth into.

'This is the end of an era,' said an important-looking gentleman as he left the church with a group of friends. He was tall and fat and kept wiping the sweat from his face and neck with a white handkerchief. A much older man replied that peace was in the air and jerked his head towards the coffin which was being carried out of the church at that moment. Walking beside it as chief mourners were Don Peppe and a stranger who was not wearing a tie. The fat man pulled a face.

'What of it? One's not worth a shit and the other's not the only fish in the sea . . . '

'Come on, let's go,' said Luciano taking my arm.

We walked out under the gaze of the public, some of whom were taking photographs. But I was thinking over what I had heard. What could it mean? No one could say that Don Peppe wasn't worth a shit, so why should they have said that he was not the only fish in the sea? I was very puzzled.

*

A few months later I was summoned by Don Peppe. He had been ill with influenza and we hadn't seen much of him around the farm. His voice was very weak and he was coughing too. Without mentioning the name I was expecting, he told me that some friends of his who had met me had rememberd me and wanted to see what I could do. He said I should feel honoured. He said that he had put in a word for me and that everyone valued his opinion. If I failed to prove myself as a man he never wanted to see me again.

'*Voscenza* need have no fear,' I said with my hand on my heart. I could feel it thumping, but I had no intention of showing my feelings, especially since Don Peppe was not alone: the farm manager was there and another man with a red moustache whom I had never seen before. The eyes of all three were upon me.

'Fine, Giovannino, fine. And your father, how is he?'

'Not well. There's no work and no money.'

'I thought as much, that's why I wanted to help. You're a good lad and you need the money. Go in peace.'

When I kissed his hand my heart had already stopped pounding like a wild thing but my mind was in a whirl. If this was my big chance, I had to grab it at all costs. It didn't matter if I risked my neck, but I had to help my poor suffering mother. I wanted to get on in life, too: I had to see the sea again, at least once, and next time I wanted to bathe in it, too.

Baffurrussu[4] told me to be in the piazza at Riesi next Saturday morning. That's all he said, but I already knew better than to ask questions. Zu Vàrtulu used to say that the purpose of asking a question was to find out something that the person you were asking had left unsaid. 'But if it was something he wanted you to know he would have told you in the first place, so what's the point of asking a lot of questions?'

I must explain that things had been gradually changing on the farm. The older men no longer treated me like a child and the younger ones were respectful. When we were having our meal at midday or in the evening, and water, salt or whatever had to be fetched, the manager would never ask me.

Don Peppe himself spoke to me from time to time in front of all the others and it was obvious that he was taking a special interest in me. And I tried to deserve such treatment, trying to 'be a man' even in small matters: I walked composedly, without running, and I never shouted or laughed immoderately.

When something needed to be done, I took care to avoid any need for a reproach and always did a little bit extra over and above what was asked. And I kept my mouth shut, never saying two words where one would do nor three where two were sufficient. I intended that everyone who saw me should know at once that I meant business, that I was a man to be trusted.

It was cold in Riesi that Saturday morning, but there wasn't a cloud to be seen.

I hardly knew the place at all. My uncle, God rest his soul, had always said that the people here were difficult and one not only had to be careful what one said but even where one looked. So when we younger lads had a day's leave and a few fifty-lira notes to spend, we took the *postale* to Caltanisetta, which was then my idea of a big city. First we would go for a walk along the Corso Vittorio Emanuele to look at the women, because there you could stare at them quite openly, and at the shops displaying goods whose use was a mystery to me. Then we would buy bread and hot *panelle*[5] and go to the cinema, always the Diana, which showed a double-bill.

These jaunts were rare and always took place in winter because in summer there was too much to do, but we enjoyed them. And if our money ran out before we got to a brothel, there was a woman in Via Firenze, no longer young and with two front teeth missing. She wasn't a real professional. Some days she worked and some she didn't, but she had a soft spot for us lads; she never refused us and, even if there were two or three of us, she only made us pay once, like a bargain pack in a modern supermarket.

Baffurrussu came up to me without a word of greeting and told me to follow him at a distance. In a street near the piazza we got into a small grey Fiat. We took the road leading towards the mine, then, when it started to go downhill, turned off to the left. The countryside was ugly, it was scattered with stones and only had the odd almond tree here and there. We came to a small house with only one door and one small window. Nobody, obviously, had been there for a long time.

'Tonight you will sleep here. I shall come to fetch you early in the morning: see that you're ready.'

'Right,' I replied. He shot me an angry glance, perhaps because he had expected me to say *'Voscenza sì.'* But I had already made my mind up about him. He was some kind of manager, but he wasn't my manager.

He took a knapsack from the car. It contained some food and a bottle of wine. Then he took a package from his pocket. Inside it there was a pistol.

'Do you know how to use this?'

He didn't explain how it worked or how to load it, only how to fire it. As soon as he saw my hand was steady and I wasn't frightened of the weapon he relaxed a bit and started to tell me jokingly about the stupid things he had seen people do with pistols, even people who should have known better.

When we had finished the second clip we sat down on a wide, flat stone near the house and he told me something I have never forgotten.

'You don't need to aim a pistol if you can get close enough. Remember one thing: if someone tells you he can hit a sparrow at twenty paces, that may be so but he can still make a mistake. At one pace, on the other hand, not even a blind man can miss: with one hand he can feel where your heart or your head is and with the other he can pull the trigger. Of course the shotgun is easier to use and has a greater range, but it's a weapon for the open countryside, you can't take it into a crowded place. But you can slip a small pistol like this into your pocket and anyone who notices the bulge will think you've got a hard-on.'

When it was time for his supper he left, taking with him the empty knapsack and the pistol. The sun was now pleasantly warm, but if I hung around outside someone might see me, so I went into the house leaving the door open. I didn't know what lay ahead of me the following day, but I didn't care. Some people I've known have had a real struggle to stop thinking about certain things, but to me it came naturally.

Perhaps I had inherited this from my father, who never thought about anything but the present moment. One evening I overheard him talking to my mother about a debt that couldn't be paid off because the harvest had been so poor. Knowing that the repayment was due in less than a month, my mother was at her wits' end: clasping her hands together and speaking softly so that the neighbours couldn't hear, she asked *'u Signuruzzu*[6] over and over again what was to be done when the time came to pay over the money. All my father said was: 'First let's wait and see if we're still alive!'

I ate the food and as soon as dusk fell began to settle down for the night. The straw was fresh and smelled sweet. Nothing protects you from the cold and damp better than straw. Best of all, they had provided me with a good thick army blanket, and what with this, the straw and the wine, I was as snug as a bug all night.

It's a Sicilian custom for the men to go to the Piazza every Sunday morning; they stroll and gossip, pay a visit to the barber, drink a glass of wine, anything to pass the time until lunch.

Baffurrussu set me down just before reaching the town, on a completely deserted stretch of road. Then he drove the Topolino on a bit further and got out and I followed him to the piazza.

As the weather was fine there were lots of people about and I had to stick close not to lose sight of him.

Eventually he stopped. There were four men standing in a circle chatting and they all turned and greeted him. After exchanging a couple of words, *Baffurrussu* took the arm of a tall, thin man wearing mourning. This was the signal we had agreed on in the car. I watched him, taking care not to draw attention to myself. He had a sly expression and eyes so small you could hardly see them. He nodded once or twice, excused himself and returned to the group.

I waited for a moment to see whether they would start walking away. They didn't, so I went towards them, clutching the pistol in the pocket of my greatcoat. Just at that moment he turned away from me and it crossed my mind that one of the others might see me and warn him. But they were too busy talking and laughing. When I was within a couple of paces I stopped and shouted:

'*Vossia!*'[7]

As he turned round I lifted my arm so that the barrel of the pistol touched his chest and fired one shot. I didn't want to waste bullets in case I had to defend myself against his companions and anybody else who might intervene.

But this was inexperience. People were too busy diving for cover, running away or trying to protect themselves to give me a second thought. Those further away who hadn't seen what had happened, first tried to get closer and then, seeing others running away, ran away too. While all this was going on I slipped down a crowded street. A young man stopped me, putting his hand on my shoulder.

'What's happened?'

'Someone's been shot,' I replied. The young man started to explain to the others what had happened; he can only have been a few feet away when I fired.

The little Fiat was waiting with its engine running.

'Everything OK?'

'Fine.'

When we got to a hairpin bend, *Baffurrussu* stopped the car and told me to throw the pistol over the parapet, then he put his foot down as hard as it would go: maybe he was frightened or perhaps he wanted to get shot of me as soon as possible, but anyway, when the road got steeper and the engine began to labour and overheat, he calmed down. We stopped to let the engine cool and to roll a cigarette. As I licked the paper he looked at me curiously.

'Cool as a cucumber, eh?'

I said nothing. We got back into the car. Up till then we hadn't seen a soul on the road.

'I only heard one shot.'

'There was only one shot.'

'How come?'

'Not much point in pumping bullets into a corpse,' I said; and the sonofabitch began to laugh.

We had to stop so often to refill the radiator that by the time we arrived within sight of the farm buildings it was already dark. As I tried to find the handle of the car door I felt something being pressed into my hand.

'Count it later,' said *Baffurrussu*. And drove away at once.

As I walked along the pathway, my hands in the pockets of my coat to keep them warm, I thought about the man I had just killed. By now he would be already washed, dressed and laid out in the middle of the room with the relatives sitting around him and the women weeping and cursing me.

Near the well lay the trunk of a fig tree that had been cut down. In the moonlight it looked just like a corpse. My mother had taught me, when I was a child, to make the sign of the cross when this sort of thing happened and Jesus would make me brave. One hand was clutching the wad of banknotes; I only wished I still had the pistol in the other, because then the tree-trunk wouldn't have frightened me even if it had started to chase me.

Notes

1. *Calogero Vizzini.* By the time he died in 1954, 'Don Calò' was considered to be the *capo* of the Sicilian Mafia even though his domain was Villalba, a farming district in the province of Palermo. He was certainly the last creditable representative of the so-called old-style Mafia which had enjoyed vast political connections and formed extensive diplomatic links with the centres of economic power and other Families both in Sicily and the United States.

2. He looks like a bright lad.
3. *Francesco Di Cristina. Capo* of the strong and active Family at Riesi in the province of Caltanissetta, he belonged to the old Mafia tradition of the big estates; when he died a natural death in 1961 there were many complaints about public offices closing as a sign of respect. He was succeeded by his son Giuseppe who, although only accepted on sufferance, became involved with the expansion of the Mafia in Palermo and took part in the massacre of Viale Lazio. Hearing that the Corleonesi intended to remove him – permanently – from the scene, he sought the protection of an officer of the *carabinieri*, Captain Pettinato. He was killed on 30 May 1978.
4. Red moustache.
5. Fritters made from chickpea-flour.
6. The good Lord.
7. Contraction of *Vostra signoria*, 'Sir'.

IV

Unlike my own village which is perched on a mountain and overlooks the valleys below, Corleone crouches in a valley with mountains towering above it. Where I was born and raised there was no reason for jollity, and I didn't hear much laughter in Mussomeli or Riesi either, but Corleone, with that mountain right on top of it, was a gloomy place: even the children looked solemn.

I already knew all there was to know about it. Everyone had heard about Corleone and the Corleonesi. But I felt I was ready for it: eyes and ears wide open, lips buttoned. I knew I was young and inexperienced, so it was a case of cap in hand and eyes on the ground. But I was not afraid.

There was a kind of doorkeeper sitting behind a table at the entrance to the Bianchi hospital when I got there. He had the face of an estate guard and the suspicious look he gave me was typical of an estate-guard trying to figure out if you've got bread and underlinen in your knapsack or stolen oranges. I asked him politely if Dr Navarra[1] was available. He didn't reply for a few seconds, but sat there looking me over from head to foot.

'What do you want with him?'

'It's private.'

So what did he do? Nothing. There we were, he sitting down, me standing up waiting for him to make up his mind in his own good time. I was tempted to teach him his manners, but a new boy has to be a bit careful about throwing his weight around. And I didn't want to offend the doctor. So I explained that I had come from

Riesi and as soon as he heard the name of Di Cristina his attitude changed. He told me to wait and disappeared down a corridor.

I had seen little of life, yet I could already recognize a bootlicker when I saw one. They think that being a janitor or a doorkeeper gives them the right to treat humble folk like dirt, but as soon as they catch sight of the manager or the landlord, they start poncing all over the place, yes sir, no sir, three bags full, sir.

It was in a hospital – the Feliciuzza in Palermo – that, a few years later, I was to come across a bastard of a male nurse who ruled his ward like a senior surgeon. A friend of mine had been seriously wounded and I had taken his wife to visit him. She was five months pregnant. We asked for news but the sonofabitch refused to tell us anything. We wanted to see him, but he said it was out of visiting hours. We asked him to tell the wounded man that we were there at least, but he said he wasn't a messenger-boy. 'Is there no pity in this place for a dying man?' the girl asked. She was weeping. And all the fellow said was: 'One villain more, one villain less . . .'

I didn't even want to soil my hands. I kicked him from one end of the corridor to the other, and with every kick he turned a complete somersault.

He was yelling all the time and calling on his mother and the Virgin, but as neither of them chose to appear, it was the doctors and patients who eventually came to his aid together with some of his fellow nurses, who tried to make out that I was mad and suggested to the most senior of the doctors that I should be put in a strait-jacket. There were three or four of these yellow-bellies all trying to give each other mutual support.

I was completely calm by now, and stood there looking at them all. 'The *signora* wanted to know if there was any pity in this place. He had none. What about the rest of you?' The doctors laughed and even the patients seemed to be enjoying themselves. I realized from the start that the nurses were trying to run the place and were generally loathed. And in fact the senior doctor in charge of the department gave us permission to visit without more ado, and as far as I could see he wasn't in the slightest bit upset by what had happened.

Dr Navarra was a really fine looking man. You could tell at a glance that he had had a good education and had never touched a pitchfork in his life: a gentleman. He was in the middle of examining two old men and asked me to take a seat. When the old men left, he came over and had a good look at me.

'So you're Giovanni . I've heard some very good things about you, Giovanni. People say you're bright. But what can you do?'

The question took me by surprise. I knew how to milk a cow, graft a vine, ride a horse, cook pasta, water a vegetable plot. But I couldn't mention such things in a room lined with books to a man who worked and earned his living without ever having to set foot in a field. Eventually I plucked up courage.

'The only thing I can do well is learn quickly anything I'm taught.'

'We shall see,' he said.

A person like that had no time to waste teaching me all I had to know. But I was growing up and beginning to understand things even without being told. In Corleone, the Doctor was the big white chief and had plenty of men to rely on: yet he trusted none of them, knowing that there was always the risk of their ganging up against him. But I was an outsider as far as Corleone was concerned. Years would pass before anyone would trust me with his secrets or even invite me home. It had been the same in my village: if you couldn't find out about a man and his family, you kept him at arm's length. The Doctor was the only man I could count on, and this is how he wanted it.

He immediately arranged for me to be given a post as watchman so that I had a monthly wage coming in as regular as clockwork. I'll explain. When someone in Sicily owns an orange or lemon orchard – which we call a garden – and wants to protect it from the attentions of thieves or vandals, he gets himself a watchman. If he employs just any old watchman he's wasting his money, but if the watchman knows how to make others respect him, the garden is secure night and day because not even the most hardened villain would dare to pee under one of his trees, let alone help himself to a tangerine.

The owner was a rich man, with a large, well-maintained estate. Every now and then I went to see him, checked if there was anything he needed done, bade him good day and went back to town. I was living in a ground floor flat owned by Bastiano Orlando, who was to the Doctor what the farm manager was to Don Peppe. I learned to drive a car and acquired a gun licence.

The Doctor gave me a pistol. It was German, but I can't remember the make. I felt very strange the first time I went for a walk through Corleone with it tucked under my armpit. Giovanni Marino, who was with me, laughed at me for cuddling it, so he said, like a baby at the breast. But after a week I was used to it. I never left the house without it, and at night I slept with it under my pillow. That pistol was my wife.

A wonderful thing happened in February. The Doctor took me to Palermo in his car. He sat in the front next to Vincenzo Cortimiglia and I sat in the back, as comfortable as you like. The thought of the sea sent shivers of excitement down my spine. Cortimiglia knew this, and every now and then said: 'Get ready,

Giovannino, it could appear any moment now.' The Doctor was amused, too. I remembered what the sea was like, but I didn't know it was like a living being, one day as merry as anything and the next as ferocious as a rabid dog. The waves were as high as houses, and terrifying because they were so close that the spray was landing on the road.

But the port was something else again. Ships bigger than I could ever have imagined, and close enough to touch. They were all rocking about on the water, some lifting up and some dropping down, and every now and then they would bang together. I said that if they asked me, those ships were going to sink. The other two laughed and the Doctor turned to Cortimiglia.

'You see how it is, Vincenzino, boys bred in the mountains . . . '

We stopped outside the Albergo Sole, in Palermo's famous Quattro Canti.[2] What a contrast with the main square in Corleone! This was a really smart place, the exact centre of the city. I had heard about it in Mussomeli, because Don Peppe went there from time to time to meet Di Cristina, Don Calò Vizzini and other important friends. The Doctor expected to be only a few minutes and left Cortimiglia and myself sitting in the car, but with so much to look at I would have stayed there quite happily for a couple of hours. There were magnificent cars, elegant women and shops which made those in Caltanissetta look ridiculous.

'Watch out, Giovannino, if you get lost here we'll never find you again,' said Cortimiglia, taking the mickey out of me. Normally I would have quelled him with a glance, but this was a special day and some things weren't worth bothering about.

Then the Doctor took us to Dagnino's for a coffee. There were great mounds of pastries under the glass counter but, as the Doctor was paying, I was too shy to say I would like to try one.

Meanwhile, I was getting the feel of the big city. Although my eyes were still out on stalks, I played it cool and held my tongue. But when we got to the Hotel delle Palme my mouth fell open. It looked like paradise, yet it was only a hotel. The Doctor was to have lunch there with a friend from Palermo.

'We'll meet again at three,' he said to Cortimiglia. I just caught a glimpse of the inside of the place: all antique furniture and walls covered with material. And the people were definitely out of the top drawer. Even the waiters were dressed like gentlemen, with black suits and bow ties, and I wondered how the customers could possibly tell who was who between waiters and fellow guests.

When we arrived back in Corleone in the late evening, the Doctor drew me aside.

'So you've seen what Palermo looks like, Giovannino?'

'*Voscenza sì.*'

'Prepare yourself for a closer acquaintance.'

I began to travel. I, who had known only the farm wagon, began to get used to motor-coaches, trains and hired cars. From time to time, I went to places like Trapani, Riesi, Villalba, Mussomeli and Favara, but more often my destination was Palermo.

To start with, they were always errands, though errands that, naturally, required discretion. About once a month, for example, I was sent to the offices of the regional council. During the presidency of La Loggia, the municipal health officer was Milazzo. I spoke to his personal secretary, always the same man. The matter was to do with the new hospital in Corleone. It had been finished since '52, but as far as I could make out, the Doctor didn't want to open it.

Sometimes the jobs were a bit special. These were nothing to do with the Doctor: Palermo was not his zone, but the men I took my orders from would be friends of his who had asked for his help because they needed an unknown face. The procedure was always the same. I would wait at a certain place – nearly always the station – and whoever came to meet me would explain what was wanted on the way. I usually worked alone. Sometimes it was a case of having a few words with the foreman of a builder's yard, sometimes it was with a council employee, sometimes with a trader: people who were trying to dodge an obligation. They soon changed their minds. Only once did I have to get really rough. The chap tried to convince me that he was not afraid of people like me and even tried to punch me. After I'd hit him on the head with the butt of my pistol, he didn't get up again. Whether he ever recovered, I never found out.

Every time I visited Palermo I invariably went to one of those restaurants with a wooden floor raised on stilts overlooking the sea in the Romagnolo district: there were dozens of them in those days. Spanò's was the best, but I was happy with any and it was always a treat: I would order *spaghetti alle vongole*, *pesce arrostito* and ice-cream, and afterwards I took my shoes off and paddled along the edge of the sea. I never bathed because there were always people around and they were all nicely tanned, whereas I, under my clothes, was white as white. Apart from which, I couldn't swim. In the winter, on the other hand, I frequented a big restaurant, a *rosticceria*, in the centre of town, and after indulging myself would go for a nice walk as far as the Foro Italico and look at the sea in the distance.

But most of my work was in Corleone itself. There would be weeks when there was nothing to do, and days when there wasn't even time to snatch a bite to eat. In June 1955, during the regional elections, I sweated more than in the hottest days of the harvest in my own village. The Doctor, who was the head of the Christian Democrats in Corleone, didn't want to hear a word about communism, and as some people had been sent to Corleone to spread propaganda on behalf of the hammer and sickle, we were kept busy chasing them away and it meant a continual scurrying from one end of the town to another, on foot or on horseback, whatever.

We had to attend every meeting that took place. There were unlikely to be problems at those held by the Doctor and his friends, because he was good at handling people and, as he was in charge of the Bianchi hospital and the Association of Smallholders and had a finger in every pie, there was always a good crowd. But all the other meetings had to be carefully watched to see who attended them, who applauded whom and who took the most active part.

Besides, the people who promised to vote Christian Democrat were not always to be trusted. For such people the Doctor had devised a brilliant system. He signed a medical certificate saying that the person in question was ill or blind and needed assistance when casting his vote. And it was always us who assisted these poor blind people.

But there were also other ways of handling this problem, and we were kept busy from dawn to dusk, dealing out promises when promises were enough and beatings when beatings were necessary. And on the evening when the results were declared we celebrated with a feast I shall never forget: it was one of the few occasions on which I have got drunk. The following morning there were a few anonymous letters sent and some unwise rumours spread by certain individuals who had been persuaded to vote the right way. The squeakings of mice. The *maresciallo dei carabinieri*, being new to the place and therefore anxious to make his presence felt, summoned me and tried to probe even more than a father confessor. Why was I living in Corleone? What did I do for a living? Why did I need a gun licence?

He also wanted to know if I had an alibi for a certain night when I had gone with some friends to 'chop firewood' in the orchard of a certain man who had refused to pay for protection. But I had alibis a-plenty and witnesses better than he was; a pharmacist, a professor, two council officials. The police station was too small to hold all my witnesses. The *maresciallo* was a big man with black hair and an enormous moustache. At the end of the interview he looked at me with eyes narrowed to slits.

'I know you for what you are, you little thug. But you can be sure of one thing, which is that as soon as I lay my hands on you, you'll feel the weight of them before I throw you inside.'

And he held up his hands for me to see: they were like paddles. At fifty years of age he still hadn't realized that hands and moustaches are no match for a pistol and that I was quite prepared to put a hole in his head there and then in memory of Zu Vàrtulu. But the Doctor just laughed.

'You're talking bullshit, Giovannino.'

'He's got it in for me. He's going to sew me up so tight I won't be able to move a finger.'

'So go home for a bit, make yourself scarce for ten days or so and leave the rest to me. Either he'll leave town or we'll put a muzzle on him.'

*

I went home to the village for a few days two or three times a year. After settling down in Corleone the first thing I did was buy a new suit. Now that I no longer worked with cows and pigs I wanted to forget about trousers made out of sacks and held up with bits of string.

But when my father saw me arrive one evening wearing my new suit, he turned to my mother without even replying to my greeting of *voscenza benedica* and asked her if it was Sunday. And my mother, as she kissed me and held my face between her hands, said very quietly so that he couldn't hear:

'Go and change, son, go and change!'

My father was right. What was the point of smart clothes? Every now and then village people who had been in America came home on a visit. Dressed like circus clowns, they strutted around all day long spouting American slang, handing out cigarettes as long as your arm and buying people coffee, then they sold off a tiny piece of land or a *dammuso*³ and vanished never to be seen again. But for the rest of us it was a different matter. If you want people to respect you, you mustn't make them gossip. What would the neighbours think of a young man who went around dressed like the gentry?

I had to be very discreet about money or my father would have been offended. On one visit I had the walls whitewashed, on others I saw to a new door, a little gas stove, wool mattresses. But I always asked him first. The biggest problem was installing electricity. He didn't want to know about it and my mother had to talk him round, very subtly, over a period of time. She was a deep one.

I always left her a little cash in secret. It was never much but it meant that I could leave with an easy mind. Old people need so little. And my father's health was slightly better now: he couldn't hire himself out but he could work our own piece of land. I went out to the fields with him and every time the same thought ran through my mind. The land next to ours was a good holding of seven *tumoli*,[4] nice and flat, with no stones and provided with a well. The owner had emigrated to France and the land was worked by his brother. He was willing to sell it to anyone who could put up the money. My father said that this was the best piece of land in the district, but he only mentioned it in passing. He had no idea about what I had in mind.

The project required money and time. But although I was scarcely more than a boy, I had already learned to be patient.

Notes

1. Michele Navarra. A doctor and a member of the board of directors of the Corleone hospital, he was a *mafioso* of the old school, more interested in prestige and appearance than in amassing a personal fortune. When he fell out with his former subordinate, Luciano Liggio, he probably underrated the latter's determination and certainly failed to realize that behind this small, misshapen man, crippled with disease, a new and utterly ruthless Mafia was already ranged. Navarra was shot while driving himself and a medical colleague along a road near Corleone during a thunderstorm on 2 August 1958. He was fifty-three.

2. *Quattro Canti*. Literally 'Four corners', this is Palermo's central square, formed by the intersection of the two principal thoroughfares.

3. *Dammuso*. Single-room, street-level dwelling.

4. Seven *tumoli*. Just under 4 (3.703) acres.

V

One Sunday morning in the summer of 1957 I was in the piazza with a certain guy called Trombatore. Suddenly he grabbed my arm and said:

'Look, that's Liggio.'[1]

I had already heard of Liggio and I was very curious about him. The Doctor referred to him as ''u immu'[2] and said that he was a jumped-up nobody who didn't know his place and needed to be taught a lesson. Years later I heard that the two men had had an argument about the construction of a dyke being planned to irrigate the land round Corleone. That may have been so, but the truth of the matter, as I see it, was different: here was a man determined to get on at all costs and not about to let anyone stop him.

I only ever knew Liggio by sight. In those days he was still calling himself Leggio, a fairly common name in those parts: one in our group had the same name but the two were not even distantly related. I doubt if I ever spoke to Liggio more than once or twice at the most, and never about anything important. But I did get a good look at his face and it was one I shall never forget. I don't know whether it was the result of hunger or disease or whatever, but you could see at once that he was a dog with no master, quite ready to go for a priest, an old woman, a policeman or anyone else.

As a child I had known a friend of my brother Borino's just like that. He had the same eyes. His name was Nino. One day, having got a slap in the face from his uncle for being cheeky, he grabbed a knife and plunged it between the older man's ribs. His uncle was four times bigger than Nino, but he fell to the ground and lay squealing like a stuck pig.

When it happened, my brother called Nino a savage, but I had been expecting something of the kind. Of course no one should stab an uncle over such a petty matter, but it wasn't the slap that had made Nino do it. Later I got to know the reason for his rage. His mother had been unmarried, one of those things that are neither forgiven nor forgotten in a village. The teacher at his elementary school used to make the class laugh by calling him *mulacciuni*,³ and, when he was angry with him, 'son of a whore'. Until one day when he hit him over the head with a stick and Nino punched him in the stomach. They threw him out then and he never went back to school.

Whenever we met we exchanged greetings but I avoided speaking to him in case it led to trouble. He was bigger than me, but I knew how to command respect. He didn't give a shit for respect, though; he didn't even know what it meant. If the mayor had accidentally trodden on his foot, he would have lashed out even at him. Nino was like that. So was Liggio at that time. When people saw him they saw a small, twisted, poor and ignorant man, and they didn't give him a second thought. But even the least of men, if he's determined enough and not afraid of anything, can do whatever he sets his mind to.

The day President Kennedy was assassinated, in 1963, I was in Palermo. I couldn't believe it. But the same rule holds for Sicily, America and the whole world. A man can be as powerful as God Almighty, but if someone has the nerve to shoot him he'll die just like anyone else. Liggio had this sort of mentality but, unlike Nino, he was also intelligent. I realized this as soon as I saw him that day in Corleone. But the Doctor, despite being so well-educated and despite the fact that he knew Liggio personally, hadn't realized it. And this was catastrophic for him, for me and for many other people.

Anyway, Liggio was starting to worry everybody. He wasn't an estate guard any longer. He had bought a fine estate at Piano della Scala for a fistful of beans, but that hadn't satisfied him so he had begun to dabble in politics and was trying to put a finger in every pie. 'You see, before long he'll be wanting to say mass on Sunday,' said Orlando, who had known him for several years. He was well known in Palermo but no one would admit to knowing him. Pretending to be minding his own affairs, he actually did whatever he chose to do, things no one was expecting. 'Who does he think he is, this tramp!' yelled the Doctor, who couldn't come to terms with someone who treated him with such a lack of respect.

To show that he didn't give a shit for the Doctor, this man (who had owned property for a good ten years before the day I first set eyes on him, and now spent much more time in Palermo than Corleone) came into the village quite openly whenever he had business there; and even if he didn't stroll up and down in front of the *caserma*, the *carabinieri* must have known he was there.

He would have been about thirty at the time: young to have got where he was. And he had already gathered a group of young men around him who hung on his every word as if it were gospel and were every bit as tough as himself. There was certainly cause for concern, and in fact, in my heart of hearts, I was very concerned. But the Doctor only ranted and raved and raved and ranted.

So, one evening Antonio Governale and I were on our way to the Doctor's house when the man who owned the 'garden' under my protection suddenly appeared from round a corner with some other people I didn't know.

He was red in the face and didn't even wait to get near us before starting to pour out his troubles.

'They've taken away my water! I'll never have water again! I'll have to plant maize instead of fruit just to be sure of having bread to eat!'

He was nearly in tears. Governale asked him a few questions, then took him to see the Doctor while I stayed with the others. Standing in the road with my hands in my pockets, listening and saying nothing, I gathered that Liggio and his cronies had cut off the water supply to the orchards and given it instead to a sheep-farming co-operative. This was a serious matter, much more serious than the fate of the tangerines these men were making such a fuss about. When he returned, Governale looked pleased and gave me a wink.

'He's a dead man,' he said, speaking softly so that only I could hear. This time the Doctor had really hit the roof.

I wasn't allowed to be involved. It wasn't that they didn't trust me, in fact I knew everything there was to know about the operation, but, as Orlando explained when I offered to help, this was a local matter and it was up to the locals to deal with it. I was to encounter the same attitude in Palermo on many future occasions: if a woman plays around it's the offended husband who pulls the trigger, not the best man or some second cousin.

That day in July was a scorcher. The Doctor had to make a long round trip to various towns and villages in the area and I drove him in his car, a Fiat 1100. He was in a very good mood and chaffed me constantly about my driving because I still wasn't altogether confident and tended to take sharp corners too slowly. It was late when we got back. Orlando was waiting for us outside the house; he was alone. The attack had failed: Liggio had got away, possibly injured.

I never found out exactly what had happened. There were rumours that the gang at Piano della Scala had been warned and were on the alert, but some said it had been simply bad luck and others chose to say nothing at all. It takes time to get to the root of a matter, but time was running out.

Orlando was evidently anxious that evening, and I was dry-mouthed with rage and frustration. But the Doctor seemed well pleased. There was a way he had of talking at certain times, clapping his hands very softly together at every word, as if in time to music. In his opinion the little jerk had been taught a lesson he would never forget. And now, if he had any sense, he should grow up.

'Still, if he's wounded I'm prepared to treat him,' he said at last. And laughed.

I was in Palermo a few days later to collect the usual package: a big red envelope that felt as if it were stuffed with banknotes but it might have been papers: the ten-thousand-lira notes at that time were as big as a sheet of foolscap. I was due to meet my contact at ten o'clock in the evening. At half past he still hadn't shown up and I was beginning to get impatient. At last he appeared, but empty-handed.

'You can go home. There's nothing to deliver.'

'What do you mean, nothing?'

'Navarra's dead.'

They'd killed him with a machine-gun, together with another doctor, on the road to Prizzi. Nowadays even the Pope gets shot at, and if Christ risked coming down from the cross he'd get shot at too, but in 1958 things were different. This seemed like something out of a western. The Doctor had had no suspicion of danger. In fact he'd set off without a care in the world. It was raining hard, too, and the road was deserted. It had all been too easy.

But that evening I knew nothing of what had really happened and no one could tell me a thing. It was too late to catch the news on the radio so I went to the station and paced up and down thinking furiously. I was half out of my mind and so desperate to know the facts that if I could have grown wings I would have flown to Corleone, even in the dark. The first taxi arrived about four, an ancient 1100. The driver said he couldn't take me that far because he was booked for seven o'clock. I argued but he didn't want to listen. I hated wasting money but this was no time to be worrying about saving it.

'Look, I'll pay anything you like,' I said. He still refused.

'A promise is a promise. It's not a question of money.'

By this time I was in the front seat next to him. I opened my jacket and let him see the pistol in its holster.

'I you won't do it for me, do it for the sake of this sick child.'

The village was seething like a cauldron. I swear that even the dogs were discussing what had happened. The place was crawling with *carabinieri* both uniformed and in plain clothes. I went straight to the dead man's house. The sympathy visit, *'u vistu*, is the same all over Sicily. The women weep and the men come and go. Everyone exchanges kisses and speaks in a hushed voice. The shutters are closed.

For the first time it occurred to me that the Doctor had not been a rich man. He had had friends, respect, prestige, but these can't be inherited. And the funeral was quite unlike that of Don Calò. People were afraid: you could sense it immediately. When one of us walked down the street, they looked at us as if we were condemned men. If the enemy had dared to remove a general, what hope was there for the foot-soldiers?

We met in an empty granary that same evening. Vincenzo Cortimiglia was the most outspoken but others shared his opinion too. I kept my mouth shut, not only because of my youth but because I was still an outsider. The Doctor on whose say-so I had been included among them was no more and I had to wait to see what my position would be now. Eventually Sebastiano Orlando spoke up. He wanted to go to Palermo and talk to friends of the Family. Only then could decisions be made. No one contradicted him. Orlando was the one with most authority now that the Doctor was dead, and the rest of us needed to be told what to do by someone who knew what he was doing.

Besides, the *carabinieri* were interviewing us all, one at a time. I was expecting them to summon me as well but it didn't worry me. Orlando had told me to explain that I was employed by him if they wanted to know why I was living in Corleone; meanwhile, one simply had to watch out and not do anything stupid. But I could see that things were changing very quickly indeed. Just when I thought that I was settled down permanently, I was going to have to start all over again.

There was another meeting when Orlando came back from Palermo. The advice had been to keep calm until things had blown over, then take stock. Meanwhile, they had confirmed their confidence in Orlando himself. As it would have been dangerous for us all to meet in any one place, it was agreed that from now on all orders and information should be passed on by word of mouth. It was two days before the August Bank Holiday. I began to feel safe again and this feeling was reinforced by the fact that the *carabinieri* had still not interviewed me although they had already grilled all the others. The reason for this was that my name did not appear on any civil or police record. If strangers are unknown they hardly exist. And I had been very careful to keep out of the record-books. Some especially.

But I was wrong to feel safe. I was at home, shaving before going out, when the terrible gun-battle, which left Marco and Giovanni Marino and Pietro Maiuri dead, occurred. We all rushed to the scene and stood looking silently at each other and at the corpses in the street, which no one was allowed to touch before the magistrate arrived. As I had been friendly with Giovanni Marino, Orlando asked me if he had told me anything special within the last few days. He couldn't believe that after the death of Navarra, with the town still crawling with *carabinieri* and journalists, anyone would have had the nerve to do such a thing without severe provocation.

His theory was that the Marino brothers and Pietro Maiuri had planned a major offensive between them and then been caught napping. This was disproved when Vincenzo Cortimiglia was also gunned down in the street, because Vincenzo's speed of reaction was second to none. He had known about my passion for pistols and had taken me out one day into the fields to teach me a trick or two about hitting a target. He really knew his stuff. And now he was dead. Everything was grinding to a halt: no more orders came, no more money, and the Doctor's friends never got in touch. Sometimes it occurred to me that only a few weeks had passed since the Doctor's death, but I couldn't believe it: every day had brought such terrible changes that it seemed more like years.

Bastiano Orlando was spirited away no one knew how. I had gone to his house very late one evening, knowing he was usually in at that time, and had been confronted by two women who looked like furies. They had been expecting him for several hours and knew that he was not the type to go off anywhere without telling them, not at a time like that. They were still trying to hope for the best, but in their hearts they already knew the worst. They chewed their fingers, cursing everything they could: the town, Sicily, the whole of creation and its Creator.

'*S'u mangiaru*,'⁴ said an old man as he passed the door. And he crossed himself.

I walked away with my eyes bent on the ground. It was too late to knock on anyone's door, but I bumped into Luca Leggio on his way home after a few glasses of wine. I asked him if he had seen Orlando.

'No, I expect he's at home.'

So much for my friends: one had disappeared God knows how or where, another had turned to drink to give him Dutch courage and I'm certain that he hadn't even got a pistol on him, and what had become of the others? Some were asleep, some were in hiding, all were waiting for the next meeting to count how many were left and to talk bullshit.

I made my decision there and then: I had to get out. Even if the others refused to grasp the situation, I saw the danger. I wasn't running scared but I didn't want to die. That same night, while I was trying to get to sleep, they tried to break into the house. Sitting in the middle of the bed, I started to fire away like a madman. I can still remember that moment. No more noise came from the street, and neighbours, hearing the uproar, stayed behind their locked doors. It was after two. I could do nothing, not even switch on a light. There might be a couple of corpses outside the door or there might be four live men waiting for me.

As soon as it began to get light, I dressed in the oldest clothes I had. I took nothing but my money and the gun. There was no one outside and no blood on the ground. I began to run, keeping close to the walls. I had been mad to wait so long! I should have got out when the Doctor was killed! Orlando's disappearance meant a death sentence for every member of the Family. And, in fact, they were all killed one by one: Ramondetta, Trombatore, Governale, Reina and the rest. Before the Doctor was cold in his grave there was no one left to mourn him.

I learnt about this later. At the time I thought of nothing except getting out of town and lying low in the open country, far away from any road.

That was thirty years ago, and I have never set foot again in that accursed place.

Notes

1. *Luciano Liggio* is generally held to be the only remaining top member of the Sicilian Mafia, which he is suspected of running from his prison cell. Born in Corleone in 1928, he first came to prominence in '58 when he murdered the local boss, Michele Navarra – a crime for which he was given life and the only time he was ever sentenced: at the Palermo trial he was acquitted for lack of evidence. Arrested in 1964, he escaped shortly afterwards from the prison hospital in Rome where he was being treated for Pott's disease and remained in hiding for ten years until he was re-arrested, in Milan. While in gaol he underwent a complete metamorphosis. The semiliterate estate guard, hunchbacked as a result of disease, has disappeared, his place taken by an elegant, assured gentleman who speaks good Italian, reads extensively and paints pictures. A recent exhibition of his work, in Palermo, aroused a great deal of controversy.

2. The hunchback.

3. Meaning both 'mule' and 'bastard'.

4. 'They've done him in.'

VI

This was the start of one of the worst periods of my life. I couldn't go back home. That would be the first place anybody would come looking for me. To hide there would have meant putting my parents in danger, and I didn't even want them to know why I was on the run.

I couldn't go to Mussomeli either. For one thing, my presence there would have compromised Don Peppe; besides, that was all part of the past and I had no intention of going back to herding calves and mucking out stables. I had discovered that I could do other things, I was a man now and that's how I wanted it to stay. Today, thirty years on, I might add something else that didn't occur to me at the time: Don Peppe would not have taken me back at the farm, and perhaps he would even have refused to hide me there. One only hides a man from the law, not from one's friends. The Corleonesi didn't rate much in a place as far away as Mussomeli, but they still rated more than me.

I thought of paying a visit to Di Cristina, since it was he who had sent me to the Doctor. But I had never been 'his' man. And what did Riesi have to do with me? Di Cristina could deny any knowledge of me. He might even do worse. He had sent me to Corleone because he was friendly with the Doctor. But what if he was friendly with Liggio? They might have been hand in glove for all I knew.

In fact, Francesco Di Cristina was a 'man of honour' in the old-fashioned sense; a type no longer found in Sicily.

He was against bloodshed and had always been able to command respect without using violence, which is how it used to be years ago. But I only knew him slightly and this I couldn't know.

I took to living rough out in the countryside. The weather was fine and I could sleep anywhere. Every so often I would go into a village in the evening, taking every possible precaution, buy essential provisions at the first shop I could find and slip away immediately. It was dangerous: strangers are always conspicuous and I could feel all eyes upon me. And things were different in those days. There were no shops in the smaller villages, and even where there were shops, they didn't sell bread because every family baked its own at home or bought it direct from the bakery, and the bakeries were closed in the evening when I got there.

Patrolling *carabinieri* were another danger on the country roads at harvest-time, and estate guards were thick on the ground. Gradually I worked out a system. Whenever possible I slept in a cemetery, because cemeteries are the most tranquil places on earth. The first time it's a bit spooky if you think about it, but I had lived long enough to realize that the living are more dangerous than the dead.

One evening, because there was a light rain falling, I slept in a family vault, but in the morning I woke to find four builders at work right in front of it. It was one of those September days that are just like July, and the heat and smell in the place was indescribable. I began to think I had been better off hiding in the tin drum in the builders' yard.

Instead of going home at lunchtime, the builders sat down under a cypress tree for their meal. I watched them through a crack in the door. They had fresh bread, mortadella, cheese, fruit and wine. A whole bottle of wine each. My desperation and hunger were keen enough to force a thought into my head: I would whiten my face with chalk, strip naked and emerge like a ghost with my arms stretched out in front of me. How they would run! Then I could eat my fill, drink their health and get the hell out of there. But that was pie in the sky, and in the end I stayed in the dark, silent vault until about six o'clock, by which time I was so thirsty that I threw myself into a ditch and drank the stagnant water swarming with frogs and tadpoles.

As soon as the weather started to get cooler, I exchanged cemeteries for churches. I had abandoned the tiny villages by now, and there were plenty of churches in the larger ones. In those days they were always open. I slipped in towards evening, taking care nobody saw me. The scene was always the same: a couple of old ladies waiting to make their confession, a few lighted candles and the rest of the place in darkness. I settled down behind an altar and slept. When leaving in the morning I had to be careful, but only one sacristan ever noticed me, and he must have been a bit simple, because he just laughed and said nothing.

I covered a good half of Sicily in my wanderings. I still remember the miserable, wretched places like Santa Elisabetta, Petralia, Delia, Contessa Entillina: they were more wretched than the village I was born in. The place where I stayed longest was Canicattì, in the Province of Agrigento: I was there for nearly three months. One night I slept in the cathedral, which instead of being in the main piazza is tucked away in a small, almost unfrequented square, and the following morning I saw a house with an overgrown garden right opposite. When I passed it again in the evening, I noticed that there were no lights on.

It was easy to enter and leave because no one lived

in the square and it was completely deserted after dark. For safety's sake I removed the bulb from the single street-light, and that was that. Then I laid in a good stock of provisions and at long last arranged a kind of bed. The only problem was the rats: they were enormous but as thin as skeletons, and not having had a chance like this for God knows how long, they threw themselves on my food, even in daytime and right under my nose. Some respect they showed! They'd even have eaten my gun given half a chance. Although it wasn't my house, I had to go out and buy poison.

The money, meanwhile, was running low. And now I had to face the problem of Christmas. If I neither visited nor wrote, my parents would become suspicious. But this was where the danger lay. Where is the most likely place to find someone you're looking for? At home on Christmas Day. After a lot of hard thinking I came up with a passable solution. I wrote a couple of lines to say that I couldn't come home, but wished them a happy Christmas. Then I went to the place where the bus left for Agrigento and began to study the faces of the passengers. I saw a man of about fifty-five or sixty dressed in the way peasants do when they go to town, and asked him if he would do me the favour of posting the letter as soon as he arrived in Agrigento. I started to explain that I had to conceal my whereabouts from certain individuals, but he grabbed me by the wrist long before I was through.

'I understand. Don't worry.'

I would have done the same in a similar situation.

On Boxing Day I left the house with the garden. By then nobody would be expecting me in the village. Because my parents were illiterate and had to ask someone to read letters for them, by now most people would have got the message. I reckoned on staying there for a couple of days and then going away again. The plan was a good one, but the trip was destined to end before it began. As I turned the corner of the road leading away from the square, I met two *carabinieri*, wearing boots and with rifles slung over their shoulders. I had just shaved but my hair was long and my clothes were in pretty poor shape. They stopped as I passed them, then summoned me back.

'Hey you, have you got your papers?'

I had. They searched me and found the pistol. They were only youngsters, and their little faces positively lit up. But their mouths fell open when I showed them the gun licence. They couldn't believe their eyes but kept looking from me to the photograph and back again. Then they took me to the *caserma*. The brigadier was Neapolitan and not at all happy about having to spend Christmas in Canicattì when he was longing to be near the sea and Vesuvius. He demanded to know why I was carrying a pistol.

'Can't you see who signed the permit? Look, the signatures of the mayor, the prefect and the chief of police. If you want to know why they gave it to me, ask them.'

'Why did you apply for it?'

'None of your bloody business.'

He slapped my face, but not hard. He saw me as a boy and thought he had the right. But I was beyond the age of allowing myself to be slapped around. I said:

'You see why I need a pistol, *brigadiè*? You are protected by your uniform, but if you weren't . . . '

They threw me into a cell. They may have wanted to check up on me, but had this gone on for any length of time it could have been dangerous. The incident taught me the wisdom of not rising to a bait. If I hadn't reacted, what could they have done to me? As I had no police record and the licence was perfectly in order, they would have had to let me go within twenty-four hours. As it was, they held me for nearly a week, contrary to the law, and from the third day on I refused all food except a little bread and drank nothing at all for fear of ending up like Pisciotta.[1] I needn't have worried: nothing happened and in the end they let me go. The brigadier never came near me.

Outside it was freezing and a north wind was blowing. As it was already New Year's Eve and there was no hope of getting to the village in time to celebrate it, I was tempted to return to the house that had been my shelter over the past week. But like the brigadier I had had my bellyful of Canicattì. And since fortune favours the mad, I got a lift in one of those old lorries with a long bonnet. The driver was a decent fellow who was hurrying home to his family. He shared his wine with me, told me about his problems and set me down in a village about fifteen kilometres from home. A good three hours' brisk walk.

It was midnight as I set off. I thought about nothing: for the moment cold was my main enemy and it took all my concentration to fight it. I had eaten almost nothing for two days and the mouthful of wine I had drunk with the lorry driver was peed out as soon as I got out of the cab. It was pitch-dark. As I walked I prayed and cursed by turns, but since neither did any good, I started to sing instead. Not a single car passed me for the entire time that I was on that road, there were no lights to be seen in the countryside and it was even difficult to make out the shape of the village on top of the mountain.

As I began the long climb, the force of the wind increased unbearably. I had given up singing: my lips were so stiff I couldn't move them. I walked with my eyes shut, trusting my feet to go in the right direction. Every now and then there was a lull in the wind which was an enormous relief: I cupped my hands over my mouth and breathed as deeply as possible. Then the wind started up again, worse than before.

There was no way I could appear on the doorstep at four in the morning, so I planned to spend the rest of the night in an old barn, long abandoned, on the outskirts of the village. Heaps of stale straw are not perhaps the ideal setting for New Year revelry, but to me they would have seemed like silken sheets!

But the barn wasn't there any more. I can't remember whether it had fallen down or been burnt down. I stood looking at the four low walls that were all that remained, then went on walking. I nearly laughed aloud when I thought of what I had come down to, I who until the beginning of August had had money in my pocket, two smart suits, and dined in the seafront restaurants of Palermo. Anyway, I found a courtyard which was reasonably sheltered from the wind and curled up in a corner. As soon as it was light I was on my way. Here and there I saw broken plates on the ground: the New Year had been celebrated by the traditional smashing of china.

When I knocked on the door, it was my father who asked who it was, but it was my mother who opened the door as soon as she heard my voice.

'Giovannino!'

'*Sabbanadica!*'[2]

She embraced me, then drew back immediately, looking at my father.

'*A frevi havi.*'[3]

I was in bed for a week. No one knew whether it was bronchitis or bronchial pneumonia. From time to time the fever subsided and I saw my mother sitting near the bed. My father, when he was around, acted unconcerned. But I know that he was worried too.

I had nightmares about two or three men bursting into the room and shooting me in my bed. But there was nothing I could do: I was too weak to care. The first time I got out of bed and sat in a chair, my mother pulled something wrapped up in a handkerchief out of the linen chest. It was my pistol.

'What are you doing with this?'

I told her that in the city the pistol took the place of the shotgun used by the estate guards on the farms. It was used, for instance, by the civil guard. Mention of the civil guard reminded her that a certain Giuvannazzu had come to the house looking for me. He was the oldest policeman in the village. He had the same name as me but everyone called him Giuvannazzu because he was fat and ugly and never shaved. I suspected that the Neapolitan brigadier had asked him for information about me, but I told my mother that it was something to do with legal domicile so that she wouldn't suspect anything.

'Was the fever very high when he came?' I asked. 'I don't remember anything about it.'

'What are you talking about? It was the beginning of November when he was here. And again a fortnight ago,' replied my mother.

I kept quiet. Picking up the pistol from the table where she had left it, I got back into bed and stuck it under my pillow. I knew that Giuvannazzu was not a man to be trusted, but I didn't dream that he was the one who would betray me to the enemy.

'Perhaps he'll come back before I go and I can say hello,' I said. My mother nodded; she was busy laying the table.

'After the holiday, he said.'

I had to get away at once. When we were eating

I told them that the man I worked for had expected me back on the day after Epiphany, so my return was already overdue. My mother, clasping her hands and with tears in her eyes, begged me to stay longer. But my father silenced her.

'He's a man now. He's got to work.'

But my country travels were over. If I had to stay in hiding, I would stay in hiding where I chose. No more churches and graveyards.

I returned to Palermo in a very determined frame of mind. The day I arrived the weather was bad, it was raining and even the sea looked unfriendly. But this time I was no tourist. I had to make a living.

The first problem, and it was an urgent one, was to get my hands on some money. I didn't need a lot, just enough to enable me to look around and make the necessary decisions without feeling pushed. I only did three jobs, all in the late afternoon and in the centre of town. First I sussed out the situation by going into the shop or looking through the window, noting where the till was and studying the owner's face. If he or she looked tough I gave the place a miss: I didn't want to murder anyone for peanuts.

Eventually I did all three places in ten minutes: a delicatessen, a dress shop and a big bar. Apart from in the dress shop, where there was nobody else except the proprietress and myself, all the customers were totally unaware of what was going on. Pistol to the ribs, a couple of crisp words, cash into pocket and a brisk exit, but not at a run. Back at the boarding-house where I had taken a room, I counted out the notes. I could live discreetly for two or three months. And that was all I needed.

Having hidden some of the money, I stuffed the

rest into my pockets and went in search of a good meal. Sitting in the warm restaurant with a bottle of Chianti on the table in front of me, it seemed too good to be true. And at night I slept like a babe. The room was too small but at least I had it to myself: all the other rooms had two or three beds in them. The owners were from Capizzi. The wife did all the work and, in my opinion, deceived her husband, who was much older than she was and a semi-invalid. Then there were two children and the husband's mother, Za Marannina.

I mentioned this because it was Za Marannina who, without realizing it, saved my life. She was a really nice old lady, and got on better with the customers than with her daughter-in-law. People who come from Capizzi have a strange way of talking: if you ask them a question, they reply with another question. Once, for example, when I asked Za Marannina where her daughter-in-law was, she replied: *"U sacciu iù*?"[4]

Anyway, I planned to go to the port the following day to look at the sea and find out if there was anything doing down there. But I hadn't yet learned about the *palermitani*. If they don't know the person speaking to them, they won't even answer a straight question. Strangers who come from anywhere outside Palermo are completely ignored, and my accent was something I couldn't disguise. I eventually returned to the boarding-house at about four in the afternoon. I hadn't actually fixed anything up, but I'd had one or two ideas that I wanted to chew over at my leisure.

The weather, which had been bad in the morning, had cleared up later, so Za Marannina was out doing a little shopping in the local stores. The poor old woman wouldn't even step on to the balcony if it was raining or there was a bit of wind. I met her on her way out of the baker's and she stopped as soon as she saw me.

'*Figghiu, turnasti finarmenti*?'[5]

'Why?'

She said that two smartly dressed young men had been looking for me all day. Naïve and slightly simple-minded, she was still quite capable of explaining things and I gathered that the men had not been policemen. They wanted to know what I looked like, where I came from, if I had gone out the day before towards evening and what time I had returned. They had also asked if I had any friends who came to see me or if I always came and went alone. Before going they had tipped the proprietress generously and given my room a good going-over. They might even have found the money, I thought, but this was something Za Marannina could not be expected to know. She kept calling me *figghiu*, son, and gripping my arm. She realized that I was in trouble but didn't understand why.

I, on the other hand, understood perfectly, and it was a bit late in the day. At least one of the three shops I had hit must have been protected and the owner, instead of going to the police, had immediately lodged a complaint in the most effective place. It had been clever of them to find me, and if they caught me now I was a dead man.

'Are they still at the house?'

'*Sì, figghiu.* Eating olives in the kitchen.'

I couldn't go back there again. All I had were the clothes on my back, the pistol and a few thousand lira. And I was on the run again. Was this my fate? To be gentleman and tramp turn and turn about? I was shaken by such a wave of fury that I was quite prepared to march into the boarding-house, take those two smart *picciotti* by surprise and punch their elegant suits full of holes with my pistol. But my ID document had been registered when I took the room. I didn't have a hope in hell of getting away with it. The attempt would have been moronic, and although I have made many mistakes in my life due to ignorance or inexperience, I have never been a moron.

I spent that night with a prostitute. No documents required. Then I found an old man who rented rooms to students, casual workers and anyone who came along. Again, no documents required.

But once again I was dead broke and didn't dare knock off any more shops. If people came looking for me and couldn't find me, they might think I had left town. But I knew that sooner or later my luck would run out. So I changed my routine. Every evening I went for a stroll in the most elegant parts of the city. Days went by when no opportunity presented itself or the opportunity, when it came, was too fraught with risk. Eventually, I managed to spot the right people every time. All I had to do was let them see the gun, nothing more. I took only money and ignored everything else. Only once I asked a man to hand over a gold watch, because mine was broken. I never took jewellery. What would I do with it? I didn't know any fences and, besides, there's no surer way of playing into the hands of the police.

But the police weren't my only concern. One evening I took about eighty thousand lira off an old couple in Via Empedocle Restivo, and the next day there was a report in *Il Giornale di Sicilia*. I was reading the paper in my usual bar: the only subjects that interested me were sport and local news. I read that the old couple were the parents of a councillor: whether he was local, regional or provincial I wouldn't know, because all Sicilian politics centred on the city and there were certain things I knew nothing about. Anyway, a big fuss was being made about the affair and the paper said that there was going to be a major inquiry, that the streets of Palermo were becoming unsafe after dark and that it was a disgrace and something had to be done about it. In fact, the police had been carrying out random checks in various bars – including the one I usually went to – and several arrests had been made that very evening.

While I was reading, the barman was discussing the matter in an aggrieved tone of voice with the porter from a local school, a man I knew. And suddenly the school porter said something which made me prick up my ears:

'That district belongs to Don Antonino Matranga. Someone's cocked a snook at him. And he won't take it lying down, you'll see.'

'Let's hope not,' said the barman. I paid for my drink and left.

I say this with all sincerity: I was still unaware of the fact that the whole city was divided into zones and not even the mice dared nibble a cheese rind without the permission of the area boss. I had never heard of this Matranga; I had certainly not intended to cock a snook at him and I had no idea that the money taken from the old couple was his too.

I counted my remaining capital. By putting both feet into one shoe I could live for six months without working. I had to make people forget about me or think that I had left Palermo. And I had to use those six months for finding out what I could do. But having thought this far, I realized how bleak the future really was. The city was vast, yet there was no place for me. All round me I saw new office blocks, new shops, businesses, dockyards; but for me there was nothing doing.

Palermo was surrounded by acres and acres of orchards: it occurred to me that I might find work there. That was a job I could do. So I began to trudge from one holding to another. I left in the morning and returned in the evening. Every time I saw a large area of cultivated land I stopped and asked if there was any work, but it was difficult to speak to the owners: either there was nobody around, or the only people to be seen were foremen or estate guards. And all of them regarded me with suspicion. 'We don't need anyone,' one of them said, while another told me to 'Be off!' The estate guards were the worst of all. One of them pointed a double-barrelled shotgun at me to frighten me. I kept my mouth shut. What could I do? If I beat one of them up, the word would be all over the place in no time at all and I could never dare show my face again.

I gave up on agriculture and went to try my luck in the construction industry. I knew nothing about the builders' trade but I could always do labouring. And there they played a different tune. Workmen were always in demand and few questions were asked. But the pay was low and the treatment rough, and to complain was to be chucked out. There was one foreman I particularly remember who had a habit of calling all the labourers *moittu 'i fami*, miserable sods, and laughing at them. He just ordered us about, shouted insults and laughed. I ignored him.

One day, we were all sitting on the ground eating when this foreman called out to me in his usual manner and ordered me to go and buy him ten *nazionali*.[6] I pretended not to hear. He was a relative of the La Barbera brothers who owned the business, and in fact I had once seen him in the Lancia belonging to Angelo La Barbera and knew that they were cronies. Everyone stopped eating and looked at me. As a child I had often been sent off on little errands with the encouragement of a box on the ears, but those times were long gone: I was no longer a child but a man of twenty-four. And it wasn't just the age that made a difference: I was determined that these things should never happen again. I hadn't left my parents alone, and fending for themselves, just to be called a 'miserable sod' by any bullying bastard.

I got up and walked away. As I passed him I pretended not to see that he had spread out a fine red napkin on the ground with bread and mortadella, wine and a pear. I trampled on it all. The other workers, meanwhile, had all got to their feet, and the foreman dared not let them see him swallow an insult like this. He started to chase after me, shouting, 'Come here and I'll kill you!' I turned round and stood with my hands on my hips, looking at him and waiting to see how he rated his chances with me. He stopped in his tracks. Still yelling and spitting on the ground, he swore that I would never get work as a builder in Sicily again, that I could starve in the gutter and he would take pleasure in the sight. And, while I stood there looking at him, he turned on his heel and made off towards the surveyor's hut, cursing every saint under the sun whose name he could remember.

An idea had been buzzing round my head for some time now. I knew it violated the code, but this incident finally made up my mind. So, when I came off the building site I went straight to the Albergo Sole. Another winter was about to begin and I couldn't survive another winter like the last. I also wanted to take some money home at Christmas. My mother had sent me a letter (written, of course, by someone else) telling me that things were bad: the roof had started to leak and the builder wanted a fortune for doing the work and supplying the new tiles.

I asked to see Francesco Di Cristina. An employee told me they hadn't seen him for months, that he was ill. But these people were not tight-lipped like the estate guards and I knew how to handle them. He told me in confidence that certain 'bookings' had been made for the end of November, though he didn't know the exact date. I gave him five hundred lira.

*

And I had a bit of luck at last. Every day I took up my position in the Quattro Canti, sitting on the steps of the town hall, from where I had a good view of the entire front of the hotel, and there I waited. When I finally saw him arrive, I was as excited as a child. Father and son were sitting in the back seats. The driver, a fair-haired lad who looked like a northerner, stopped to let them out and then drove off. I waited a while longer because I wanted them to finish all their business first.

The car reappeared at about four o'clock. I went into the hotel ahead of the driver. Di Cristina was talking to a group of men, but one could tell that nothing serious was being discussed. I went up to him. His face, marked by illness, had aged. I kissed his hand.

'*Voscenza benedica, Don Cicciu.*'

He looked at me and his eyes narrowed. His son, Giuseppe, also looked at me but without recognition. The other men were now standing slightly apart, still talking among themselves.

'You got away?'

'*Voscenza sì.*'

Don Cicciu explained quickly to Giuseppe who I was and why he was surprised to see me. I could have cut capers out of sheer joy: I hadn't expected to be greeted so paternally. And I didn't know at the time that there was a decided coolness between Di Cristina's family and Liggio.

'And how are you managing now?' he asked at last.

'I have to manage as best I can, now that the Doctor's dead. I get by . . . '

'And do you want to stay in Palermo?'

'*Voscenza sì.*'

'You're mad! It's a death-trap!' he exclaimed, and

beckoned to one of the other men who had broken off his conversation and was looking at us.

'Dino, come here; I want you to meet this young man . . . '

The driver was waiting outside with the car, sitting on one of the mudguards. When father and son had taken their places in the car and everyone was raising a hand in a farewell salute, I noticed Giuseppe looking at me through the half-open window of the car. His steady, penetrating gaze was that of a hunting dog pointing at a pheasant concealed in the undergrowth.

As soon as the car had driven off, the man Don Ciccio had called Dino said goodbye to the others and then turned to me. He was a man of about thirty-five. Although he said nothing, I could see that he wasn't too happy with the introduction. But no one refused Francesco Di Cristina. Walking up and down on the pavement he began to fire questions at me. He wanted to know exactly why the Doctor had employed me, what I had been doing since his death and how many times I had been *'nta argia*.[7] I replied never.

'You've got a clean sheet?'

I could see he didn't believe me, but I wasn't worried: things like that can be easily checked. At last he gave me an address.

'Go along after the holiday.'

He meant the holiday period around Christmas, and there was still a month to go. It didn't matter. One thing I did not lack was patience.

Shortly before that meeting at the Albergo Sole I had met a girl. She worked as the cashier in a restaurant in the city centre which I patronized from time to time when I was in the money. I've always made friends quickly and easily, but I hadn't had much practice with girls.

Where, after all, would I have had the opportunity? On Don Peppe's farm? In the Canicattì churches? The only period of my life when I had lived in anything like a civilized style had been in Corleone; but in those days that was a place where to wink at a girl was more dangerous than to insult a man while he sharpened his knife on a whetstone.

Her name was Nuccia, a form of Giuseppina. All the customers tried to chat her up when they went to pay their bills. I wanted to be different: good morning or good evening, nothing more. But I watched her all the time while I was eating, and although she noticed, she pretended not to. One of the things I liked about her was that she came from a village in my own home province.

One night I arrived when the restaurant was already closed and the grille lowered. Nuccia was crossing the road. I noticed that a man was following her and trying to force his company on her. As soon as he attempted to take her arm she stopped to shake him off and I was at her side in a twinkling. I couldn't believe my luck in being presented with such a heaven-sent opportunity.

'Run along home; it's getting chilly and you might catch cold,' I said to the boy. He looked harmless enough: he was wearing glasses and had the face of a child. But he wasn't about to give up that easily. He came a step or two nearer, keeping his hands in his pockets.

'And who do you think you are?'

'Someone who's about to punch your nose.'

He went off without another word, but when he got to the corner of the road he turned round and shouted an insult at the girl. Then he broke into a run. I wanted to go after him, but Nuccia stopped me with a shake of her head.

'Let him be,' she said. I realized that she didn't want

to encourage me too much, afraid that she might only be exchanging one nuisance for another. I gestured towards the square where she seemed to be heading.

'I you will allow me, I should like to see you to your door.'

'Thank you, but actually I live just over there.'

She was pointing to an old, dark building on the opposite side of the square. I replied that if she had no objection I should still like to accompany her.

'You're very kind.'

Unstuffy, but nice. Just how a girl should be.

But I had problems at that time. The restaurant was not a cheap place, so I could only afford a coffee when I went there, and I walked from where I lived to save the bus fare. Whenever possible I waited for her outside in the evening and we walked the short distance from the restaurant to her home together.

She lived with her aunt. Her father was dead and her mother had three younger children, all girls, to provide for, so this aunt had offered her a home and had found work for her straight away because the proprietress of the restaurant was a friend of hers. So Nuccia got her meals and accommodation free of charge and sent all the money she earned home, not even keeping back a thousand lira for herself. A girl in a million. Girls like that are rare even among country people, and much rarer in a city such as Palermo.

At Christmas she went home for a few days and I stayed in the city. I didn't want to go home empty-handed, and also I wasn't sure that a visit to the village would be safe for me. I wrote that I couldn't get away for the moment but would come later, though I gave no precise date. And the day after Epiphany I kept the appointment at the place I'd been told to go to.

The person I was looking for wasn't there, and as I didn't even know his surname, the fellow I saw looked at me very suspiciously. He relaxed a bit when I mentioned Di Cristina but still wouldn't tell me anything. So I went back the next day, and the day after, and the day after that and so on for a whole month. I was desperate by now, and had to do two jobs just to keep body and soul together. The second time I very nearly came unstuck. The man put up a fight and I had to punch him on the nose. Then, as I turned the corner, I saw a police car, an Alfa 1900, which happened to be patrolling. Seconds later they had found the man and the siren was wailing. I slipped into a haberdasher's.

It was a few minutes before seven and the *padrona*, an old lady, was alone. She was frightened that I was going to rob her, but when she realized I meant her no harm she became most cooperative, closing the shop early and pulling down the blind. While we waited she told me about her son who was in prison for something he didn't do: in fact she called the judge an incompetent bugger. Before I left she wished me good luck and poked her head out of the door to make sure the coast was clear.

Don Ciccio's friend turned up at last: his name was Bernardo Diana. I kept mum about the number of times I had had to make the trip before seeing him, and he turned out to be much more friendly than I had expected. He said that he could probably find something for me to do as long as I didn't expect too much. The only problem was that the natives in Palermo didn't like strangers. But seeing that I had worked first for Don Peppe Genco Russo and then Dr Michele Navarra, and seeing that I had been sent to him by Don Ciccio Di Cristina, they might make an exception in my case. As long as I didn't expect too much.

'I won't.'

I was to go every morning to a bar and billiard-hall in Via Villagrazia where I would be told if there was something for me to do.

'I needn't explain the rules to you because you learnt them in Corleone. Our rules here are the same. Any special regulations I shall explain whenever necessary.'

He gave me some money straight away. Not much, but it was a lifeline for me at that particular moment. He also had a cup of coffee brought to me.

'I know you're having a rough time at the moment,' he said. I realized that he had done some homework. That was the reason he'd avoided seeing me earlier. I said that things would look up if I could find somewhere to live: I needed a room in the centre of town. He laughed.

'In the centre of town? Sure, why not try the Politeama, you can sleep on the stage. This isn't Corleone, you know, where the cats and dogs sleep in the same bed. *This* is your town centre. This is where you find your home, your friends and your work. Get it?'

For seventeen months I had been an orphan. Now I had a family once more.

Notes

1. Gaspare Pisciotta, a cousin and lieutenant of Salvatore Giuliano, died of poison in prison in 1954.
2. God bless you!
3. He's feverish.
4. How should I know?
5. My son, are you back at last?
6. Cheap cigarettes.
7. In the nick.

VII

Two years flew by. My job was that of *spicciafaccende*, a chaser-up of other people's problems, but the missions weren't confidential like the ones the Doctor had given me. It was mostly a case of talking to friendly council employees and arranging licences, permits and things of that nature: matters of administration.

My wages were paid through a draper's shop where I was down as a delivery man. My home was on the top floor of an old palazzo. It was only one room but it was a good size and I had a fine terrace all to myself. It was fun cooking outside in summer on a little gas ring, and it reminded me of the times that my father, my brothers and I had cooked our meals out in the fields. Except then, after the meal, I had slept on the ground with the ants crawling over me, but now I had a splendid wool mattress and the sheets were always clean.

After a year I began to be given a different kind of work. I saw Diana every now and then and each time I hinted, with all due respect, that I was capable of better things if they would only give me the chance to prove it. He either said nothing or cracked a joke at my expense. But on one occasion he told me to do the job I had been given and stop being a pain in the backside. And he wasn't joking.

Then one day they sent me to a building site on the Messina road. From Monte Pellegrino today you look down on a city like New York, but in those days there was nothing, and the most powerful Families were throwing themselves into the construction business and scrambling for building permits and land to build on. Sometimes labourers and foremen who had dreams of becoming contractors would get there first. If the size of the job was fairly small, they paid their dues, the *pizzo*, and were allowed to get on with it. But for things on a larger scale they had to team up with the contractors who mattered or, in certain cases, quit the site.

No one spelled it out to me, but the first time I set foot on a building site I understood the drill. First, someone would pay a visit and make an offer. If the offer was not accepted, I went along with a warning. What happened after that I don't know, though sometimes I read about it in the papers.

I thought they had chosen me for this job because I knew how to make a good impression and was generally capable. Later I learned the truth: given that there was always a risk that the owner of a piece of land or the foreman on a building site might turn nasty or even draw a gun, and that this could result in the police becoming involved, then someone like me with a clean record could deny everything and stand a better chance of being believed. Anyway, I was gathering experience by the day. In no time at all I knew exactly what I had to say to the person I was dealing with as soon as I saw him. And if words were not enough, I let him see the butt of the pistol and swore on the Immaculate Virgin that if he so much as lifted a finger I would blow his nose clean off his face.

Everything went like clockwork. I was always sent on these missions because when I was involved there were never any complications. 'You're the final demand chap,' Diana said on one occasion. And even though he said it jokingly, I could tell he was pleased with me for never disgracing him, having been responsible for employing me in the first place.

The owners of land scheduled for building were easy to deal with. Building-site operators were violent types, every one of them ready to knife his own brother for the sake of a minor contract, but the owners of land were just normal decent people: peasants, impoverished aristocrats, members of the professions. Their faces went white as chalk and they tried to argue about the price and get me to see reason. They were completely wet behind the ears but not dangerous. Indeed, it was best not to frighten them too much or they might do something silly. So I told them all how to protect their own interests. 'These people don't mess around,' I would say, and give them to understand that I had seen many a good man and true end up in a hole in his own land, the spot marked not by a headstone but by a fine ten-storey block of flats with lifts and every mod con.

These stories never made copy for the press, and I never had to teach any of these people a lesson. But where building contractors were concerned, I quite often had to deal with men who thought all their problems would be solved by getting rid of me. I remember each one of them: names and faces. I usually only saw any of them once. Several died with their shoes on, maybe a day or two after my visit. Two or three went on to become famous, owning hundreds of apartments, orchards or building plots, with large sums of money in several banks and friends in parliament.

For the first two years I was never involved in any action. Once only I took a wounded man to the 'spitaleddu.[1] I was in my usual bar late one evening when a light green Fiat 600 drew up outside. Behind the wheel was a certain Antonino, a chap about the same age as me. We drove to a part of town where I had never been before and where another, bigger, car – whose make I don't recall – was waiting for us. We were to act as *pruvulazzu*.

Pruvulazzu means 'cloud of dust': it makes everything invisible. When a sensitive load is being transported and there's a risk of road-blocks, a car goes ahead ready to assist. At the first sight of a uniform it creates a diversion: a skid, a minor accident. Then who's going to bother about the car behind?

We arrived at a large building on the very outskirts of town. It's not there any more: the area has been completely built over. But in those days there was a fine courtyard with steps leading up to the door and an Alsatian chained up outside. At that late hour all was dark and silent. There was a doctor, a real doctor with a properly fitted up surgery complete with a couch. He had two women helping him: one might have been his wife, the other was a nurse. They were evidently expecting us. I had never seen the wounded man before. He was covered in blood, but because he was wrapped in several blankets against the cold, it was impossible to tell where he had been shot. He was whimpering like a child, it was dreadful. The doctor and the two women went to work without saying a word. Unknown to them, of course, all their care for the wounded man was going to be in vain because he was killed six months later.[2] When we were on our way out, Antonino gave me a nudge in the ribs.

'Have you made mental notes about this place, Giovannino?'

'Why?'

'You should, because one day you may have to come here alone.'

'But would they let me in? They don't know me from Adam.'

'No one comes here uninvited,' said Antonino. 'It's our own hospital. Ever seen a hospital refuse admission to a wounded man?'

Every Family in Palermo had its own first aid post. It

had other things as well, but for the moment I was told no more.

Meanwhile, I had asked Nuccia to marry me. Her aunt knew all about it, but because she felt responsible for the girl her only concession was to allow us to stay out a bit longer after work – and to go for a short walk on days when the restaurant was shut, but never after dark. We went to the Botanical Gardens or the Villa Giulia, places often used by courting couples.

As we were not yet officially engaged, we had agreed to say nothing to our respective families, but a month or two later I had a chance to see my mother. Francesco Di Cristina had died – on the Feast of St Joseph, his son's name-day.[3] There was no way I could stay away from the funeral. I had been devoted to Don Ciccio, a real gentleman and a 'man of honour' in the old-fashioned sense of the word. I had not received the long-term generosity from him that I had from Don Peppe during the years on the farm, but those years were long gone. Don Peppe was ill, he was seldom seen and the *carabinieri* were persecuting him. I dared not even go to see him to thank him for what he had done for me; it would have been too dangerous for both of us. But Don Ciccio Di Cristina had made a man of me by his introduction to the Doctor, and had rescued me from poverty by his introduction to Bernardo Diana. I had to accompany him to the graveside at all costs.

The service was even more beautiful that Don Calò Vizzini's at Villalba. Maybe people had shown greater respect on that occasion, the veneration due to a great patriarch; but at Riesi I saw more affection, a whole population in mourning. All the schools and offices shut as a mark of respect. I heard later that the papers were very critical about this, saying that it was a scandal, a disgrace for the whole of Sicily.

They didn't know what they were talking about. If a bishop or a mayor on the take had died instead of Francesco Di Cristina, they wouldn't have called it a 'disgrace' for a whole town to attend the funeral. But it wouldn't have happened: people only mourn those who are worthy of their love and respect, who have done good to others and been everyone's friend. That is why I went to Riesi that day. He had done things for me although he hardly knew me, and had asked for nothing in return. You don't find men like that nowadays. The world has changed.

Throughout the day I waited for an opportunity to speak to his son Giuseppe. When the moment arrived, I expressed my sympathy and asked him if he remembered me. He had a good memory, like his father.

'I live in Palermo. You can always find me there if I'm needed,' he said. One of the rules of the honourable society is that if one respects the father one also shows respect to the son unless he forfeits it. He looked at me with the same steady gaze I had noticed that day outside the Albergo Sole.

'What is your name again?'

'Giovanni.'

It was still early that evening when I got to the village, but there was no one at home. Neighbours told me that an aunt, my father's elder sister, had died. So I went to pay my respects and we all came home together. It was very cold.

'You don't have to go back again straight away like you did last time, do you?' my mother asked. I could have stayed for six months and she still wouldn't have been satisfied.

'Tomorrow.'

My father said nothing. The next day he got up early as usual but stayed at home, telling me the latest news about his work and the people we knew and meanwhile roasting the occasional olive on the fire. Before the meal he had to go out for a moment to see the saddler. That was all my mother was waiting for. She examined my face carefully and asked how I was. She told me that I had lost a lot of weight, that I didn't look well. A skinny lizard.

'Aren't you ever going to get married?'

The timing was perfect. I began to laugh, and she laughed too, smoothing the shirt over my chest with her hands.

'*Cchi cc'è, figghiu miu. Cc'è ccosa? Cùntami.*'[4]

"*U nenti 'un c'è*,"[5] I replied. I didn't want to say anything definite as yet, but I was pleased to have dropped a hint at least, and it made my mother happy too, and when my father came back with some sausage wrapped in the butcher's yellow paper, he found us as merry as a couple of crickets.

'How can you laugh when we're in mourning?' he demanded. But I knew him well enough to tell he was not really angry.

Notes

1. The little hospital.
2. This may have been Vincenzo Maniscalco.
3. 19 March.
4. What is it, my son, is something in the wind? Tell me.
5. Something's up.

VIII

1963 was a year of disasters. Everything that happened was going to hit me like a hailstorm, yet, knowing nothing of the situation in Palermo, I was blind to the fact. All I heard was from friends chatting in bars; but even they said little – with the excuse of being *uomini di panza*[1] but really because little was all they knew. Now I can explain what I saw.

The year before, in December, the government had invented the Antimafia. Had this happened a year earlier, nobody would have noticed because things were going well and there was general agreement. But the situation in Palermo had changed drastically between '62 and '63. Although there was still plenty of money to be made from contraband, the big money was in building. The city was growing and there was a great shortage of land. There were also highly profitable contracts to be won in the public sector, but to get one's hands on them one needed to have friends on the district councils, the regional councils and in Rome, and those who had such contacts guarded them jealously.

In January they did away with Totò La Barbera. 'What has become of La Barbera?' the papers asked. 'Is he dead? Is he in hiding? Has he been kidnapped?' They were all looking for him. But even I, who was nobody at the time, knew that he was dead. His brother knew this too, because a few days later he blew up a car in front of Totò Greco's house.[2] Up until now, TNT had only been used to scare a few contractors into remembering their manners. Quite a few nice cars were to go the same way over the next few months.

Don Peppe Genco Russo was arrested the same year. The news hit me like the blow from a clenched fist; it was as if they had arrested my own father. I knew that he was an old man by now and no longer counted for anything. They hadn't dared touch him when he could have shown them what he was made of, so in the end they put the handcuffs on a semi-blind pensioner. That Don Peppe was no longer a force to be reckoned with was something of which I, too, was aware. Money had destroyed the old ideals of respect. In the past he hadn't even needed to speak to be obeyed; now he didn't need to speak because no one would have listened to him anyway. But because his name was still known to everybody, they had put him in prison to show that they had the situation under control.

In the early summer a friend persuaded me to bathe in the sea for the first time. His name was Salvatore but he was called *Cascittuni*, which means someone always too ready to shoot off his mouth, to say more than he should. We went to Mondello. The sand was scorching, I was hopping about from one foot to the other, and he was laughing. The sea was nice and calm, which was just as well because I certainly wouldn't have ventured in otherwise, but even so, every time a wave lapped against my stomach, the shock of the cold and my fear of the water made me yell.

I didn't attempt to swim. *Cascittuni*, born and bred in Palermo, dived in to show me how clever he was and teased me for standing there shivering with the water up to my belly-button. Who knows, perhaps, given time, I might have learnt to swim. But on 22 June they murdered Bernardo Diana. It happened in the evening, the gunmen firing on him from a Giulietta as he drove with a friend in a Fiat 500.

Nobody was expecting it. Throughout the next day and most of the following night I had the feeling that what had happened in Corleone five years before was about to happen all over again: the whole Family would be massacred one by one with no chance of defending itself. For me the alternatives were a wooden overcoat or taking to my heels yet again. In the event, neither of these happened: the men who had gunned down Diana were identified and would pay the price in due course. But at the time I didn't know this, nor did I know what was expected of me. Without Diana I had become an outsider again. If he hadn't spoken about me to his superiors, I was back to square one and could retrace my steps to the Albergo Sole.

One evening, while I was in the bar, a man of about forty came in. I had long ago given up the habit of standing with my hands in my pockets watching the billiard players; now, even when my mind was busy, I watched every unexpected arrival carefully, was wary of cars stopping beside me and after dark never used the same street twice in succession. In short, my eyes were doing the job they were intended for.

As soon as he saw the stranger, the barman nodded in my direction and the man came over to me without hesitation.

'Giovanni?'

I said yes without hesitation, knowing at once where he came from even though I had never set eyes on him before. I won't reveal his real name as he's in prison at the moment and I don't want to make things worse for him. I'll call him Cosentino.

'Listen carefully, *picciotto*,' said Cosentino, and without wasting words he explained what I was to do, where

I would find him, how I should behave and all the rest. There was a need for men of action and I could become a good one. The days of wrestling certificates out of the council and carrying messages to building sites were over.

He still wanted to know whether I had relatives who were *carabinieri*, customs officers or traffic wardens. Because although a man may be trustworthy, if there is a rotten apple in the barrel you never know what might happen. Then he warned me that it was mortal sin to touch another man's wife or sister or the daughter of a friend. To screw a man's wife is like pulling a gun on him, and you only pull a gun on enemies or strangers, not on one of your own kind, not ever.

He wanted to know if I was a man of my word.

'If you don't give any promise it's all the same to us: everyone's free to choose the life of a man or that of a dog. But if you can't keep it don't give it. Once given, stick to it or else. It's all or nothing.'

This was the morality required of a man of honour. Cosentino knew that it was already engraved on my heart, but he had to spell it out all the same because I had never taken an oath. I have seen many oath-taking ceremonies since then, always involving new *picciotti* full of enthusiasm. Even the most determined were over-awed, and how could it be otherwise? The room would be in almost total darkness, the words spoken as solemn as any uttered by priests at a Lenten service, and every face would look forbidding and mean. But although the *picciotti* thought they were promising something, this is not what the *giuramento* is about. I understood this, being older than them and knowing what was going on. It is a threat. The men sitting around the table aren't saying: swear to be loyal for all time. They're saying: if you are disloyal you will die.

The whole conversation only lasted ten minutes. I

was quite happy about it, but he had a warning for me:

'Remember that you're an outsider here. You know what that means?'

''*U sacciu*. I know.'

'We trust you,' said Cosentino, but I knew that I would have to earn this trust daily, every morning as soon as I opened my eyes, before drinking my first cup of coffee.

But meanwhile I had set my mind at rest. I felt I was on firm ground again and could walk in safety. This was naïve: the worst was yet to come. On the thirtieth of the same month came the great Ciaculli[3] cock-up: 'Another Giulietta gone for a Burton,' as a man I saw every day in the bar described it.

So the state, which had minded its own business up to now, decided that it was time to show that it had balls. Because everyone was talking about the massacre and the press was moaning and calling for justice, it licensed raids by night and day and I was picked up in my own bar, thrown into a tiny van with fourteen others and taken in for identification and interrogation.

It was the first time I had been arrested. I felt quite calm and, as for the pistol, I had the licence for it. But given the situation and the sort of people I was dealing with, nothing could be taken for granted: since the war had broken out in Palermo, not even the officials were sticking to the rule-books.

First they took down my personal details. It was like being tested by my teacher: a series of questions and answers, but when I got the answer wrong I got my face slapped instead of being rapped over the knuckles with a ruler. It was nothing much, but only my father had ever hit me before without getting hit back. The interrogators were a brigadier and a marshal, though the latter came and went as he had other customers to deal with in the neighbouring rooms. Then a *commissario* came along, one of the old school. 'You don't come from this stinking city,' he said, 'so why risk your neck for the others?' And then: 'I can see you're a man of intelligence. I can push you under or throw you a lifebelt. It's up to you.'

This didn't work so I was hit again. They were convinced – or pretended to be – that I was behind the killing of Bernardo Diana because he had refused to cut me in on a deal involving contraband cigarettes. This made me laugh so they hit me again. And then they accused me of the murder of a certain Corsino, a water guard. This was sheer bullshit, but of course there was no way I could recall where I was on that particular day or what I had been doing. All I could do was deny it, so they went on hitting me.

At one point the marshal told the commissioner that the best thing to do would be to let me go with a pat on the shoulder and a big thank you, so that my associates world assume that I had 'sung' and would promptly eliminate me. The inspector disagreed, saying that I had so much on my slate already that nothing in this world stood between me and a couple of long stretches. This was the only time I felt really afraid. If word actually got around that I was a traitor, it would be all over with me. They would have thought: 'Of course, he's an outsider . . . ' None of this showed in my face. I didn't have much breath left by this time; I just said:

'OK, if you've got evidence, hand me over to the magistrate and there's an end to it.'

That night I thought about my parents. If I were declared guilty with or without proof, my old mother would die of grief and shame and I could never look my father in the face again.

But instead of a magistrate, it was a lawyer who came to see me. Although I had never set eyes on him before, he had been retained to defend me. He's now a respected criminal lawyer: in 1963 he was barely thirty but already had what it takes. He made no comment about the bruises on my face. He spoke courteously, never raising his voice, never letting go of the lawbooks in his hands, the *articulari* as they are called in Palermo. He asked me if I had confessed to anything, and if there were eye witnesses. Afterwards they released me unconditionally, though they suspended my gun licence. The lawyer took my arm and told me I looked knocked up. I must rest, he said: a couple of weeks at home nice and quiet, with no work and no visitors. '*Sulità santità*: Solitude is healthy.'

'I understand.'

'Good chap. Is there anything you need?'

What could I possibly need? When they arrested me they had also arrested several poor bastards who weren't involved at all and a few petty criminals who didn't have the price of the next meal. They, too, had been threatened and punched about, but I had a lawyer, a home, and no need to work the moment I got out of the hands of the law. There's an old proverb that says: '*Cu è riccu d'amici è poviru di guai*: Many friends mean few sorrows.' And I certainly had friends, friends who could protect me even from justice, the so-called justice of the Antimafia Commission which pretended not to be able to locate Liggio when he absconded, who searched for enemies of the state in our bars rather than in the council chamber and then locked up Genco Russo, who couldn't even blow his own nose, so that the people who read newspapers could see pictures of an old man hand-cuffed and feel happy.

I saw these things happening at the time but it was only after many years that I understood, and it is this understanding that I need to communicate now. The memory of the blows has faded with the years, but I still remember how I slept when I got home. It was late evening when I went to bed, and when I woke up it was evening again.

But there was no way that life was going to be peaceful for long, because at the beginning of the autumn, in Corleone, more of the Doctor's men who had so far managed to stay alive, God knows how, ended up with wooden overcoats. One of them was called Streva. I had assumed he was dead already, but apparently he had stayed there, rubbing shoulders with the men who had massacred all our companions.

This meant that nothing had been forgotten, that someone from Corleone might come knocking on my door even five years on. I told Cosentino about it. Unlike poor Diana, he took nothing lightly.

'Streva and the others weren't members of a Family. Where you're concerned, no one would dare harm you.'

This was just what the manager had said when I was working on the farm. But even though only a few years had passed, those days were part of a previous existence. I still didn't know Cosentino that well and didn't want to take liberties, but I couldn't stop myself from replying.

'They harmed Dino Diana, though.'

'But those weren't real men.'

'Not real men of honour?'

'Not real men. Some things should never happen, yet from time to time they do. Wasn't Jesus killed? Who would have thought that possible? Would you honour the scum who did that with the title of real men?'

I still wasn't convinced, and he wasn't the type to go into detailed explanations. But in his own way he was a man of honour of the old school. Not the same brand as Don Calò Vizzini or Don Ciccio Di Cristina, but a city version. Like them, he had nothing but contempt for the new mafiosi who had neither rules nor principles.

Types like the La Barbera brothers who controlled the centre of Palermo. Everyone was afraid of them, and to justify this fear went around saying that they were mad. They were mad enough to take on the Greco family in Ciaculli despite the Grecos' strength and the fact that they had too many friends. It was their fault, Cosentino said, that certain stories which would only have made the local press before, now ended up on the front page of the *Giornale di Sicilia*. And when some things get talked about too much, it means someone's slipped up. This was the reason why they got rid of Salvatore first, by burying him in cement on a building site belonging to the Geraci family, and then Angelo, *Anciluzzu* to his friends, who was poisoned in prison with the connivance of a couple of warders.

Types like Michele Cavataio.[4] I was taught not to speak ill of the dead, but he was a bloodthirsty brute, he had a twisted mind and positively enjoyed certain things. When I first knew him he was still friends with Pietro Torretta and you could tell that he intended to get to the top at any price. I was beneath his notice, a nobody, so I was able to study him whenever I saw him without attracting attention. I heard the things he said and the way he said them and it was this made me realize that I should never be a *pezzo di novanta*.[5]

Not only because I was an outsider; things would have been no different had I been born in Palermo. I was crazy about my fiancée, respectful towards my parents and wished to remain loyal to the Family that had accepted me, in the same way that I had been loyal to the Doctor. I liked walking by the sea, chatting to people and many other things too, partly because I was young, partly because it's my nature.

I once saw Cavataio leap out of his car in a terrible rage because another driver hadn't braked to let him pass. The other man, who must have been well over fifty, was wearing a hat and looked like a bank clerk. Cavataio threw him to the ground and nearly kicked him to death without even taking his hands out of his overcoat pockets. And when he was tired he spat on him and shouted that he could cash that in at the bank.

I watched what was happening and thought of the day when the Doctor and Cortimiglia had taken me to Palermo. A motor cyclist had shouted 'Bastard!' because we nearly knocked him off his bike and I was about to scramble out of the car to smash his face in, but the Doctor only laughed and Cortimiglia, also laughing, had gripped my arm to hold me back. 'Hey, Giovannino, what's this? Are you going to kill him just like that, on the spot?'

Cavataio and his ilk had no feelings for friends, or the sea or the Family. It was people like him who killed without even looking to see whether there were women and children present, who packed cars with TNT and loosed off with machine guns with no thought of the consequences for their own or other Families. Men like him, Filippo Marchese, the La Barbera brothers and many others, became successful in only a year or two by using fear. No one trusted them. No one knew what they thought or what they did. They were wild beasts.

All the same, Cosentino was proved right: no one came looking for me. I was careful and always kept my eyes open, but I never had the feeling that I was being watched or followed. Even the police stopped bothering about me and there was no problem about getting back my gun licence. I was a 'suspect person' but they had nothing on me and my record remained clean. But when they arrested Liggio and many more of the Corleone *cosca*,[6] all capable *picciotti*, at the beginning of 1964, this did more for my peace of mind than all Cosentino's assurances. I didn't reckon that any of them would be behind bars for long, but while they were they would have enough on their plates not to bother about me. So, as I was now approaching thirty and enjoying life, I decided that it was time to get married.

But of that, more later.

I was now earning reasonably well. I had stopped working for the draper's shop because, after eighteen months or so, it had closed down. When this happened, Diana had given his permission for me to go into business with someone from Bagheria manufacturing lead pipes for the building industry. I would go along to the small outfits run by people who weren't protected by influential friends and explain that our pipes were the best available. It was money for old rope, even if the money was not that good. Then my associate died in a road accident while riding his Lambretta.

In the meantime, however, I had been promoted to Cosentino's *decina*[7] and things had changed. There was a lot of dealing in contraband cigarettes in Palermo at that time. I never even got to see the big consignments: I was merely sent to set up the contract or provide an escort, and if everything went well and a good price was agreed, someone would slip me a few ten-thousand-lira notes. But where smaller consignments were concerned there was a bit more licence and the *picciotti* selected to do the deal arranged it with the owner of a boat who had to collect the cases offshore and pay for them immediately. Only once did the boatman get caught by the coastguards, leaving us empty-handed. Usually it was plain sailing: there was never any trouble with the lorry transporting the stuff, and nice crisp notes would be waiting for us at the end of the journey. It was easy: it was just a shame that we couldn't repeat the process three times a week.

But this was a less frequent perk for me than for the others. Cosentino had a high opinion of me, but he couldn't single me out for favours, being obliged to give preference in certain matters to the older men and the native *palermitani*. However, every now and then he would send me to someone who needed a reliable go-between. Nothing heavy. Squabbles between traders and farmers, the punishing of a theft or other misdemeanour, that sort of thing. The fee was by agreement and the money went straight into my pocket. I could usually manage to raise the ante by hinting – without being too specific – that the operation had been dangerous and difficult, that I had found myself at the wrong end of a gun. But that was the most I could do about the price: when a man asked for your protection, even though he was only a paying customer you had to treat him as a friend.

The fact was that the war had ended by now and a period of easy money was starting for everyone. The whores in Via Roma were charging ten thousand and the men who performed the three-card trick would accept no bets under a thousand. But I didn't even bet on the cards. As a matter of fact, it was precisely my dislike for cards that gave me a good idea. With permission from Cosentino, I and a friend called 'Nzino, Vincenzo, went to certain bars where we knew gambling was going on and pretended to be the police. Raids and identification drills were old hat; we knew just what to do. Names, surnames, confiscation of cards and money. It was always easier when there was a back entrance, because at the first hint of police everyone fled. We could have fun with no need to resort to strong-arm tactics because the gamblers were small fry and the bars had no protection. Once we found nearly eighty thousand lira on the table. So my savings grew nicely.

I didn't spend much, either. I saw men no different from myself who would spend in a night what they earned in a month. I couldn't do that: I had seen too much poverty at home and in the village, and, besides, the memory of my flight from Corleone was still depressingly vivid. If anything like that happened again, I would stand a better chance of staying hidden and living comfortably for as long as necessary if I had something to fall back on.

I did, however, buy myself a car, a pale blue Fiat 600 in good condition. How could I ever describe what a car meant for the son of peasants who until the age of ten had slept in a stable and eaten onions dipped in salt? I washed it every other day, and when I drew up outside the bar I felt like the Cavaliere arriving to visit his farm at Piano di Maggio.

My one regret was that I couldn't take it home to the village. My father had already been embarrassed at my turning up smartly dressed: what would he do if I rolled up at the wheel of a car? There were plenty of them around in the village, owned by people employed by the council, the hospital or the tax office. But when I went there I was still a peasant and my father's son. No car had ever been seen in the courtyard where our house stood. What would people say?

For myself, I couldn't care less, but while this attitude was fine in Palermo, it wouldn't wash in the village.

Notes

1. *Uomini di panza*: men of intelligence, discreet.
2. Accepted signal between *mafiosi* of an account to be settled.
3. The massacre of Ciaculli (a town in a region dominated by the Grecos), in which seven policemen were killed by a car bomb. The Antimafia Commission was set up as a direct result of this incident.
4. *Michele Cavataio*. Born in 1920, Cavataio became the boss of Acquasanta and a ruthless killer, earning himself the nickname of 'the beast'. He died in the shoot-out that came to be known as the massacre of Vitale Lazio when several men disguised as policemen entered the premises of a business and shot him and three other men. He is believed to have been responsible for the massacre of Ciaculli.
5. One of the big guns, the top people.
6. *Cosca*: a Mafia cell.
7. A Mafia 'militia' unit, comprising ten men.

IX

We were married in Cefalù. My village was too far away and, besides, my mother was embarrassed about the house being so small and wretched. And where Nuccia lived it was unheard of for the bridegroom to travel to his bride's home town for the wedding, so heaven knows what people might have thought. Customs differ, and in Sicily every village has its own.

Distance and the cost of travelling meant that very few of my relatives were present. My sister Gina wanted to be there but her husband couldn't get the time off work. On Nuccia's side there were lots and lots of women. It was a family of females: they all seemed to produce girl children and then become widows. This meant that most of them, old and young alike, were in mourning and people were murmuring that this was bad luck. I'm not superstitious but once, in her village, after I had been formally presented to her family and at a moment when no one could overhear, I did tell my fiancée that I trusted she was going to let me see forty at least!

My mother had a new dress for the occasion; my father wore the same dark suit that he had worn at his own wedding. It had been altered from time to time, but his shape had hardly changed during thirty-five years of marriage. They were both happy; I could tell that my mother was because she cried non-stop. My father just looked solemn. Still, I saw him looking at me every now and then, and when it was all over and we were about to get into the hired car, he embraced me and said:

'Now we expect a grandson.'

I had invited a dozen of my friends from Palermo and Cosentino had agreed to act as my best man. There were two Fiat Giuliettas at my wedding and other nice cars as well, so my relatives were impressed. But one thing I had not been expecting was a present of five hundred thousand lira. It did not come from him nor from the other *picciotto*, each of whom had given what he could. It came from someone I didn't know as yet. Indeed, I didn't even know of his existence at that moment, much less that he would come to be more important in my life than Don Peppe at Mussomeli, Don Ciccio at Riesi or the Doctor at Corleone. I knew that the present was a special honour, and when Cosentino slipped it to me secretly I was almost moved to tears.

'Thank you with all my heart,' I said as I embraced him.

'It will make it easier for you to set up house.'

I would have given a year of my life to be able to take my parents to one side and show them that bundle of crisp ten-thousand-lira notes, but this would have been against the rules, and I would not break the rules even for my parents. I satisfied myself by pressing a small sum into my mother's hands as we said goodbye. But that was what I always did.

We stayed in Cefalù for four days, sunbathing on the beach in the morning, enjoying a good lunch of fresh fish, then getting out and about in the afternoon and evening. That was our honeymoon.

As I said, the war was over. The consequences were, however, still being felt. Don Peppe Genco Russo had been interned in northern Italy, in a place where no one wanted him. They had sent him to cope with contempt, he who had lived and grown old surrounded with respect.

I never saw him alive again and I couldn't even go to his funeral when he died.

The police continued to arrest people without evidence, just to show they were still there and that the law was still a force to be reckoned with in Sicily. Some were people I knew about by hearsay, like the Rimi brothers from Alcamo, Gaetano Filippone and Vincenzo Nicoletti – who I saw once in Pallavicino, the zone he commanded. Others were men I knew personally or by sight. One of these was a friend from the Corleone days, a certain Bonanno. I heard that he had thrown in his lot with the Corleonesi: that was why he had survived for so long. Many of the Corleonesi were arrested too, such as Leoluca Bagarella, a stalwart and very well-known *picciotto*, Criscione, Sparacio and others. They also arrested Pietro Torretta, who had been friendly with Cavataio and was a power in Palermo. And finally, at the beginning of May if I remember rightly, chief constable Mangano managed to get his hands on Liggio, who was hiding out in Corleone. I still remember the photograph that appeared in the papers: Liggio's eyes starting from his head, and Mangano puffed up like a turkey-cock.

'So, Giovannino, nothing to worry about now, is there?' said Cosentino that same evening. He was being ironic. There was everything still to worry about. Liggio was ill and everyone knew that he only walked with great difficulty, but he had two strong arms, and even today, when he is fit and walks normally, those arms are still stronger than his legs. His right arm is called Totò Riina; his left arm, Bernardo Provenzano.[1] At that time they were free but wanted, today they are still free but wanted. You can keep a man in prison all his days, but if his 'arms' are at liberty then he, to all intents and purposes, is at liberty too.

How could I not be worried?

But, in fact, it was the police who persecuted me. They had had enough of seeing me walk about freely without a care in the world, and had decided that it was time to do something about it. So one evening they came to my house to search it. I was out. When I got back I found Nuccia as white as a sheet and too frightened even to cry. She kept asking me: 'What do they want with you?' And there was I trying to cheer her up, cracking jokes, telling her there must have been a mistake and that I would go round to the *questura*[2] and create merry hell. Who did they think they were, barging into people's houses? But she was unconvinced; she realized something was up, but didn't know what it could be.

'If you were a mechanic or a baker, the police wouldn't come here. But what is it that you do?' she kept asking. In the end she calmed down a little and went to sleep, but even in her sleep she was tossing and turning and muttering out loud. I decided that it was time I came clean to some extent, so the next morning I told her that because I had been kicked out of my job and couldn't find another, every now and then I gritted my teeth and did a bit of smuggling just to make ends meet. She swore that she would count the money a hundred times over before spending it and not spend another lira on herself so that I wouldn't have to do these things any more. And she made me swear on a crucifix that I would give up smuggling cigarettes. It made me laugh to think that I could give her that promise with a clear conscience. I hadn't smuggled cigarettes for a long time. Women are like small children: a little lie is all that it takes sometimes to make them happy.

During those days I learnt the difference between being a bachelor and a family man. Cortimiglia had warned me back in Corleone: 'A man of action must be free. Wives and guns don't mix.' I knew he was right, but good God, what kind of man is a man without a wife and family?

Three days before Christmas Cosentino told me to stick around at the Eden bar all afternoon and wait for him. At around four o'clock a man I already knew arrived. His name was Tano. He was a young man who always wore beautiful clothes and never said much. When he was with friends he played billiards; otherwise he would order a beer and sit looking at his reflection in the mirror behind the barman. He never liked starting up a conversation. Whenever we met I would greet him fairly formally, he would return the greeting and that was that.

Cosentino arrived shortly before six. At that time he was driving a bright red Fiat 128 which he kept spotless, so you could see him coming a mile off. As I came out of the bar Tano came out behind me. This was rather irregular, but Cosentino had already parked the car and was coming towards us with a broad grin on his face. He asked if we already knew each other and insisted on buying us each a coffee before we left. As I was the elder I sat in front beside him, and as we drove he told me that Tano and I were *la stessa cosa*, of the same Family, and that the time had come for us to do a job together.

'You haven't made any firm plans for Christmas yet, have you?' he asked. He was laughing.

When we stopped for petrol I noticed that the tank was already half full which meant we were in for a long drive. And in fact we took the road towards Trapani. There was no autostrada in those days. When we were somewhere near Calatafimi, Cosentino warned us to keep quiet and concentrate on the road because we had to memorize it.

We were on the road to Salemi, but we didn't go as far as Salemi itself. At the first crossroads he gave us time to make mental notes, and again at the second crossroads. It

105

was dark and we couldn't see much, but there was always a signpost, a wall or a tree that would jog the memory. The road was narrow and we met no one. Then, having passed an abandoned workman's cabin, we stopped.

'That's as far as we go tonight,' said Cosentino. 'Next time you must carry on for another kilometre and turn into a little road on the left. After fifty or a hundred metres, leave the car parked so that it can't be seen from the road and continue on foot. You'll have a walk of half a kilometre, at a rough guess. There's a plantation of carobs and a building that's visible in the daytime but maybe not at night. Anyway, carry on past the plantation and up the hill. You'll find a tumbledown cottage with a sheep pen in front. The man living there is on the run.'

I assumed that the man was a friend of ours who was hiding there with permission from the Salemi men. But it looked as though his days were numbered and perhaps he had no suspicion about it. In fact, as Cosentino turned the car, he told us there was no problem.

'He's quite unsuspecting. Thinks he's as safe as houses.'

As soon as we were heading back towards Palermo, Tano asked him when the job was to be done.

'Christmas Eve.'

The next day I bought a little present for my mother and posted it. I had been going to ask for permission to visit her, but this was now out of the question. Then, thinking I might have to use my car for the job, I spent the afternoon making all the necessary checks. But in the evening I received a telephone call telling me that they were going to let us have an *innocente*.

An *innocente* is a car that is used and returned immediately so that not even its owner is aware of the fact. Friends in the car repair business provided these vehicles; they knew exactly when the owner of a certain car being repaired was away, when he was due back and if, in the meantime, there was any danger of his wife or anybody else turning up to enquire about it. So you can drive around in an *innocente* without a care in the world and, even if you're stopped at a road block, you can always spin some yarn about having borrowed it from a friend. Once back in the workshop the mechanics check it, turn the speedo back and top up the tank. If anything really untoward has happened, the car simply disappears and is reported stolen which, in a city like Palermo, where even lock-up garages are regularly broken into, is nothing out of the ordinary.

When the doorbell rang on the morning of Christmas Eve, I was still asleep. I wasn't expecting anyone. Tiptoeing to the door, I looked through the spyhole: it was Cosentino, with his hands in his pockets and a cigarette in his mouth. He had never been to my flat before. Although he was a man who enjoyed company, and was anything but a snob, he never visited any of us at home.

Nuccia was away. I had driven her home because her mother was ill, promising to join her on Christmas Day. She had wanted me to get there on Christmas Eve, but I had made up some excuse.

'Did I wake you up, Giovannino? I know it's Christmas tomorrow, but it's a bit late to be still in bed, isn't it?' said Cosentino as I let him in. I explained that I wanted to be well rested before the night's work and he nodded.

'Good lad, just what I came to see you about. Tano will pick you up outside the bar just before eight . . . '

It began to rain around noon. I thought about the road running through the carob trees, of the mud, the dark and the cold. Even in Palermo, with the mildest climate in the world, it was cold, but up at Salemi it might well be snowing. I put on a heavy jacket with a hood, but decided against boots. I had a pair of gumboots in the cupboard, bought from a shop near the cathedral which sells army surplus stuff; but how could I appear in the Eden bar on Christmas Eve wearing gumboots?

Tano arrived on the dot. He was sporting extremely elegant patent-leather shoes and a light raincoat.

'You're dressed on the light side, aren't you?' I said. He shrugged.

'It'll clear up, you'll see.'

But it didn't. As we got further away from the sea, the rain became heavier and heavier and the windows steamed up every five minutes. Tano drove much too fast for such narrow roads, and when we got to the first set of crossroads he overshot them and then snapped at me when I pointed it out to him. He was probably getting worked up at the prospect of ruining his patent leather shoes.

By the time we started walking, the rain had stopped but we had thick, slimy mud underfoot and it was difficult to stay upright. I had brought the gumboots with me in a plastic bag and changed into them in the car. Tano had a pocket torch but we decided only to use it at the very last moment, inside the hut. The only problem would be the door, but Cosentino had said it was more or less off its hinges and a good kick would be enough.

There was a moment when the clouds parted and a bit of the moon appeared: it gave enough light for us to see where we were, but there was no danger of our being spotted because there were only two windows one of which was bricked up and the other nailed shut. The hut was a coffin. Tano looked at me.

'All set?'

I told him we should attack the door together, then he could shine the torch on the target while I fired.

'Better still if we fire together,' he said, and walked towards the door. With both hands full he could only push against it with his back, but it swung open as soon as he leant against it. There was a whiff of stale, wet straw.

Tano put the torch on and shone it around. I was right behind him and could see him clearly enough, but to be on the safe side I grasped his shoulder, put the barrel of the pistol against his neck and fired twice. He seemed to fly through the air, fetching up against the far wall. The torch broke as it hit the stone on the floor. I had a lighter with me; afraid of setting fire to the straw, I had to hold it high and couldn't see much, but it was enough to show me that half his head had been blown off.

Luckily it wasn't my job to clean up. In Salemi someone would have gone to bed early, ready to set off on Christmas morning with a plastic dustbin bag the property of the Salemi urban council – as I had done a couple of times when I was younger.

On my way into Palermo I stopped beside a phone box. Cars passed by carrying people home tired and happy after their Christmas Eve dinners. Cosentino answered the phone. Even there I could hear cheerful voices and the cries of children.

'I'm sorry it's so late, but I wanted to wish you a Happy Christmas.'

'Nice of you to remember. Thanks, Giovannino. The same to you and your wife. How are you, well?'

I told him I was fine and had been to a good party. The man from the garage was waiting for the car outside my door when I got home. I went straight to bed, afraid of going down with flu; I was also anxious to be with my wife as early as possible in the morning.

But I couldn't sleep. I wasn't thinking about Tano: I had hardly known him, he was no friend of mine. But I thought of Cosentino's trick and the detailed orders he had given me. I thought of the car, which had been consigned into Tano's keeping, signifying that he was the one in charge of the operation. He must have been a dangerous individual for them to have arranged things as they had instead of getting him outside his own front door in the usual way.

Or perhaps it had been necessary to make him disappear without trace so that those who wanted him alive wouldn't know what had happened. The one certain thing was that Tano had had no inkling about it. That was the thought that kept me awake. Tano was no fool, but he had not had the remotest suspicion that he was a marked man. The same thing could have happened to me had our roles been reversed. Now I knew that it could happen to me, on Christmas Eve, Easter morning or any other time.

I had imagined that it was the man holed up in the hut who was unconscious of his fate. But, as it happened, there was no one in there and it was Tano who was unconscious of his fate. Cosentino had explained it all to me that very morning in my flat:

'He doesn't suspect a thing. He's as calm as calm. And you must try to stay calm too. Pretend that there really is someone hiding in the hut. Get him to go in first and shoot him in the head from behind to be on the safe side.'

I had followed instructions and Tano was dead.

Notes

1. *Salvatore Riina* and *Bernardo Provenzano*. Invariably mentioned in the same breath, these two reputedly ruthless killers were both sentenced *in absentia* by the Palermo court and have been in hiding for many years. On behalf of Luciano Liggio, they run the Corleone Cosca which, over the past ten years, has become completely predominant.

2. Questura: municipal offices for the administration of all matters concerning public order.

X

As soon as I reckoned that I had enough money, I decided to buy the *setti tùmmina*, the piece of land next to ours which I always thought of by that name because it was exactly seven *tumoli*. I had to act quickly because from hints dropped by the owner's brother I knew that some other neighbours were also interested.

My mother-in-law was going to hospital for an operation and was staying with us in Palermo. There were many reasons why I did not want to take Nuccia with me, and this was a perfect excuse. Not even my mother saw anything odd in my turning up at home without my wife: it's always the daughters of the family, married or not, who have the traditional duty of looking after the health of ageing parents. But she immediately began to ask me why we had not yet started a family. She must have raised the same question ten times during the three days I stayed at home, every time we were on our own. I got sick and tired of it.

Saying nothing of what I was up to, I went to look for the man who owned the land. He told me that the others had got no further than talk, so I realized that with cash up front we were in business. Peasants are always slow to reach decisions and always afraid of making a mistake. But he knew that I worked far away and had no time for messing about, so as soon as he saw I was prepared to pay he agreed and we drank on it. I took my father to the notary. He was bewildered rather than convinced by what was happening. He couldn't make himself grasp the fact that when he set foot on that land next day he would be walking on his own property. Then we went to a dealer and sorted out another mule, a young beast with a nice quiet temperament. My mother cried for joy and put a good chunk of meat into the pasta and beans.

But my father couldn't manage a mouthful. It's no good saying that men must be men whatever happens. The poor old man who had been a servant all his life had suddenly become the master. Poverty and the need to go cap in hand to ask for favours were things of the past. Never again would he have to hire himself out by the day, and if he didn't feel like going out early on a cold winter's morning no one would call him a *lagnusu*, a shirker. How could one expect him to be hungry? He looked at the food and sighed. My mother looked at him and wept. And I sat there between them clutching my spoon and not knowing what to say. Then he began to talk about all the things he wanted to do on his new land, beginning with the boundary fence that he would grub up at once with a mattock. When we eventually went to bed, he kept tossing and turning and I heard my mother tell him from time to time to relax and get some sleep.

In the morning we went to the fields together. My father was hopping about like a cricket, a sight for sore eyes. He kept saying 'Look at this! Look at that!' and pointing out things that I had known all my life. We caught sight of the people we had beaten to the deal: two brothers, one sickly with a face like a corpse, the other short and as strong as a bull. We could see they were angry even from a distance. They hardly greeted us. I noticed that my father was upset by this.

'*Vossia* must take no notice. They're only jealous.'

'*Mah*,' he said, looking unconvinced. It was the first time ever that anyone else had been jealous of him.

*

Now I'm free to talk about it. For ten years, until he was killed, I was Giuseppe Di Cristina's lieutenant in Palermo.

In that he was his father's son, I already had reason to be grateful to him. From time to time, when I went home alone, I went round via Riesi on my way back, and if he was there I always found a welcome. He was a powerful man by this time: I heard that he was friendly with members of parliament and ministers too; even so, he never put on airs with me. Indeed, as he hadn't known of my marriage at the time, he now insisted on giving me a belated wedding present.

And then, one day towards the end of '68, he touched on a serious subject. He said that he might need me for an important job, something requiring the highest degree of confidence. I was so embarrassed at having to refuse that I hardly knew where to look. It is absolutely forbidden to carry out a job for any Family other than one's own. He started to laugh.

'Did you think I would ask you to be a traitor? Me of all people? Don't worry, Giovannino, your *capo* and I are like brothers. I'll have a word with him and you'll see.'

'Do you mean Cosentino?' I asked. He laughed again.

'Hardly! He's a *uomo di valore*, a very reliable operator certainly, but the *capo* is Stefano Bontate,[1] didn't you know that?'

There was no way I could have known. I had knocked about a bit by this time and knew better than to gape like a ninny, but all the same I didn't know what to say and Di Cristina explained the situation.

He told me that I had seen Stefano Bontate, the son of Don Paolino Bontà (as everyone called him) at the funeral of Don Calò Vizzini: he had been one of the pall–bearers. He said that Don Paolino had always

113

suffered from diabetes and Stefano looked after him with a devotion rare in a son. Meanwhile Stefano had studied and got a degree in law from the University of Palermo. At twenty he was already a *figghiu di parrinu,*[2] so much so that the Family had decided to make him the *capo* now that Don Paolino was too ill to carry on. And it had been a wise choice, because the young man had shown himself to be a capable leader.

He also explained something which I had only half realized. I was a special case. A member of the Family, but in the sense of being an adopted son. He used the very term: adopted son. Not a blood-relative. The fact that Stefano didn't know me and I hadn't even known that he was the *capo* proved it. And this was a vital distinction. I never got to know all the members of the Family which numbered a hundred and sixty according to Cosentino. And nobody talked much about them to me.

'Do you see now?' he said at last. 'You're a special case. You rank lower than the others but you're less restricted. So there's no need to worry.'

It was immediately apparent that something had happened. Scarcely a month later Cosentino took me to a place outside the city I had never been to before. There was a fine orchard of mandarins and there too was Stefano Bontate. This was the first time I had ever seen him. I thanked him for the wedding present he had sent me and at the same time devoured him with my eyes. He must have been a couple of years younger than me, very natural and not at all solemn. He spoke even better than the Doctor, like a really educated man, and I didn't even know the meaning of some of the words he used. Even Cosentino, that worldly-wise old man, showed an impressive amount of respect. And when it was his turn to speak, Stefano listened carefully and never interrupted him once. Cosentino said one thing on that occasion which made me feel very proud: he described me as a *uomo d'azione di prima*, a first–rate operator. And Stefano replied that he had guessed as much as soon as he set eyes on me.

When I went home that evening I was feeling cock–a–hoop and Nuccia kept asking what had happened to me. After her mother's death on the operating table she had become sad and withdrawn. That wasn't the only grief, either: she had become pregnant at last but miscarried almost immediately. The doctor at the hospital had explained to me that her uterus was that of a child and it was unlikely that she could ever have a baby. I told her nothing about this, but she must have guessed because from that moment she stopped knitting baby–things. How could I tell her the reason for my happiness that evening?

Whenever he was in Palermo, Di Cristina now sent for me. We chatted and he asked me questions, sometimes about matters concerning the Family. There was nothing malicious in these questions, however, and the friendship he claimed with the Villagrazia *cosca* was borne out by events. He told me that I had made a good impression on Stefano and that there would be a job for me before long. He was right, even though the part I played in the operation wasn't exactly what I had expected.

A lot of big trials were being held at the time. Although I've never been one to read books, I kept a close eye on the papers and missed nothing that might concern me. From Catanzaro to Bari, however, the men who got off were much more numerous than those who were sent to prison. And those who were sent down – maybe even by design – were men who had lost the battle even before being sentenced. Take Pietro Torretta and Angelo La Barbera, for example. For them, freedom would have been a death sentence. But Michele Cavataio, Liggio and the majority of the Corleone *cosca* got off completely or with only light sentences.

Having lived in Palermo for so many years, I had come to learn many things, and I knew that all the *capi* were agreed about one thing: Cavataio was responsible for the 1963 war. When I heard of his release my first thought was: 'He won't be around for long.' A couple of days later I was present during a conversation in the car between Cosentino and Mimmo Teresi.

'So he's going to be twisting our balls again,' said Teresi. Cosentino, who must have already known that something was in the air, turned and looked at him.

'Well, I know how men like him wind up.'

'Oh yes? How?'

'Dead.'

And it was only ten days later that Di Cristina turned up to attend a meeting. Cosentino, Angelo Federico, a member of our Family that I'd never met before and one of Di Cristina's men that I had seen on various occasions were also there. Cavataio's demise was being prepared and there were *uomini d'azione*[3] present from every Family. It was decided that they should be disguised as policemen or customs men. Di Cristina and Bontate, however, had a secret agreement to form a second group which would step in and finish the job if the first lot bungled it.

We were told to watch Cavataio's house. Put like that it sounds fairly mindless: if he survived the shooting it was anyone's guess where he would go to hide. And that was Di Cristina's opinion. But I reckoned that Cosentino had a point. The group in uniform would be using machine guns. Whatever the outcome, shock–waves would be heard all over Palermo; not even a smart alec like Cavataio would imagine that only a quarter of an hour after the attempt, and with the streets crawling

116

with policemen, more people would be waiting ready to start all over again.

'There'll be three of you,' said Di Cristina. 'One of my chaps, one of Stefano's and one who's a bit of both, which means you. Do your best.'

'*Voscenza sì.*'

'I wanted to put you in the first squad, but it's generally accepted that you're the personal property of Stefano, and I needed one of my own men, someone who everybody knows is one of my own men. Do you know Caruso?'

'*Voscenza no.*'

'A chap with real balls. You'll be hearing more about him.'

And indeed I did hear about him later, but not in the way he had in mind. He disappeared from the area where he had been interned and the police wasted a lot of time trying to find him. He had been silenced with a salt–water gag.[4]

That Di Cristina should have preferred to use another man didn't offend me in the least; on the contrary, I was flattered that he had seen fit to explain why. Still, I always reckon that a man, like a dog, should only have one master, and my master was Stefano. If Di Cristina threw me a bone I'd wag my tail, and if he told me to 'Go away', I'd have obeyed at once; but if he and Stefano had ever had a scrap it wouldn't have been Stefano that I bit.

Well, that's enough of that. On the evening of 10 December we settled ourselves in a new Fiat 125 that had just been stolen. It was cold but we didn't dare keep the engine running to heat the car because it might have attracted attention. We didn't chat because we didn't know each other. Cigarettes kept us going until nine o'clock. By that time Michele Cavataio was already dead, and although we had no means of knowing, we guessed as much. It was Giuseppe Di Franco, if I remember rightly, who came to give us the news eventually. The wait was over. The man the papers called 'the beast' had met the fate he deserved. Some journalists wrote that it was a revenge killing for Bernardo Diana, but that was only an excuse to shift all the blame for the killing on to Stefano. Six years is an unusual length of time to wait for revenge. Not impossible, but unusual.

The truth was that Cavataio was too dangerous to everybody. No one could sleep easy with him around and everyone wanted him out of the way. As far as I'm concerned, if there is any truth in the story that he ordered the killing of poor Diana, then I'm only sorry I didn't have a chance to put a bullet in him myself. I never forget people who have helped me in a difficult moment. It makes no difference that I know Diana took me on only as a favour to Don Ciccio Di Cristina. If it hadn't been for him I should have done time like any common criminal, and that is always the start of a very slippery slope.

At the end of the summer something happened that was totally unexpected and highly embarrassing. I no longer had to hang out all day at the Eden bar waiting for orders but spent most of my time with Cosentino or with other friends, taking care of my various interests in and around the town: cigarettes, of course, but there were also some shops and I was involved with a business that bought high quality citrus fruit and exported it to Germany. And whenever possible I went to have a look at the sea.

To be brief, I popped into the bar one evening for a beer. The owner had died of a heart attack the previous year and there was a new one, younger but quite bald. And in fact that was his nickname: *Testa munnata*, 'Baldie'. He told me a girl had been asking for me, that she had been in three times.

'Who is she?'

'How the hell should I know?'

I went off and thought no more about it. But on Sunday he mentioned it again.

'Is she pretty at least?'

'Terrific!'

I puzzled over it for a time but had no idea who it might be. Women seldom came to these places, nor was it a red–light district. A few days later, when I had the chance, I raised the subject.

'Have you seen her again?'

'I can see her right now.'

I turned round. She was sitting at a table on her own and all the customers were looking at her out of the corners of their eyes while they pretended to be talking or playing billiards. I hadn't seen her as I entered because I had gone straight up to the bar counter. When I went over to her, all those who knew me began to clear their throats and wink.

'I hear you were looking for me, *signorina?*' I asked politely. She was definitely one of the modern generation with her short hair and make–up. In Sicily, if a girl has the kind of face that gives you to understand that she is a homely, family type, the sort that doesn't spend her time gossiping, the kind of girl who will either find herself a decent boy or nothing, we call her a *facci di mugghieri*, a 'wifely–faced' girl. The one sitting at the bar was no *facci di mugghieri*.

'Do you mind if we go outside?'

Another chorus of coughs, low whistles and the scraping of chairs as I followed her to the door. We walked towards my car. Everything seemed normal enough, but I kept my eyes peeled just in case. As far as I knew, women were never used for life–or–death missions, but there's always a first time.

As it turned out, this matter was something quite different.

'I'm Tano's girl.'

This was a turn-up for the books and no mistake! She told me that she hadn't seen him for a long time and she was very anxious. Could I tell her anything? Caught completely off guard, I searched desperately for words. Eventually I said that I knew Tano had disappeared from circulation, but why, since we had never been close friends, had she come to me for information?

'He told me that you were going to do a job together. I never saw him again.'

Here was a right problem! If I denied it and Tano really had told her something, she would have smelled a rat immediately. If I admitted it was true then I should have to go into more explanations and one thing would have led to another, as one says. I had to say something, however, so I told her that we were involved together in a deal: a consignment of American cigarettes that had to be delivered to a particular person in a rush. But in the end nothing had come of it.

'So you don't know anything more?'

'Absolutely nothing.'

Driving very slowly, we were passing through the district of La Favorita[6] at the time. As soon as she heard me say that, she burst into tears. I gave her my handkerchief, and I still didn't even know her name. She refused to be comforted, but gradually calmed herself down.

'I must find him. And if he's dead I must know how he died and who killed him.'

I left her outside the door, noting the address, and went straight to Cosentino. I found him with Mimmo Teresi, discussing a knee operation. Teresi treated the matter as a huge joke and said that if I had my wits about me I could make her forget all about Tano. But Cosentino was furious. He could not for the life of him understand how someone like Tano could leak information to any bit of skirt.

'*Ma vidi 'sta panza 'i canigghia!*'[6] he said two or three times over in a low voice. Teresi cut the discussion short. He told me to find out all I could about the girl. If she was a danger she would have to be dealt with.

'What's her name?' Cosentino wanted to know.

'Lucia. She lives in Vicolo Castelnuovo.'

'Whose district is that?'

'Pippo Calò's, I think,' replied Teresi.

'So what's the problem?'

'Why should there be any problem? She's a broad.'

I didn't like what I was hearing. If problems were going to crop up over this affair, they would be mine. No doubt about it.

Notes

1. *Stefano Bontate* or *Bontade*: the son of 'Don Paolino', he stepped into his father's shoes while still a very young man. A law graduate and much less violent than other bosses in Palermo at the time, he was considered the key figure of the so-called moderate wing. Buscetta and Contorno both stated in evidence that he believed to the end that even the worst situation could be resolved by negotiation. He was killed by shots from a Kalashnikov rifle in April 1982 as he returned home on the night of his birthday.

2. Son of a priest: man of sound reputation.

3. Gunmen.

4. Drowned.

5. *La Favorita*: large public park.

6. What a blabbermouth!

XI

The year 1971 was the most tragic year of my life. I was thirty–six and as calm and carefree as a man in early retirement. But in the space of just two months, everything changed.

The year had begun well. Business was satisfactory and everything was going smoothly. I bought another car, a second–hand Giulia that looked like new, and my wife and I made a deal: I would teach her to drive and she would teach me to swim. The first part was easy, but as for swimming, I had convinced myself that I should never manage it, not now, not ever. There are some things which if you don't learn as a child you never will. And I was put off by remembering what had happened to a friend of mine called Reitano. He had died the previous year bathing near Messina. Congestion of the lungs. You can't mess about with the sea.

May saw the killing of the public prosecutor Scaglione. This was unprecedented. Even I, ignorant as I was, knew that magistrates were untouchable. And Scaglione was no ordinary country magistrate, either, but an *eccellenza*, a member of the senate. I heard Stefano say: '*E ora chianci 'u giustu p'u piccaturi*'.[1] He meant that a lot of people were going to suffer because of something they had had nothing to do with. The press threw themselves on to the story like a pack of bloodhounds. I read what they wrote and every line worried me more than the last. This meant trouble. And trouble was the last thing I wanted. Nuccia was pregnant at last, and this time it looked as if we were in business.

I had been worried at first, knowing that because of her under-developed womb she might have problems carrying a baby to term. But as the weeks passed and nothing happened, I began to think that I might become a father at last. And I chuckled to myself. To be on the safe side, however, I wouldn't let Nuccia go out, even on to the balcony. We had arranged for her younger sister to come and stay. She was unmarried, being as ugly as sin, but a good girl who managed everything very capably. So, even though the Scaglione affair meant that business in Palermo was suspended, things weren't too bad.

On the tenth of July, however, I heard my father had died. I rang for permission to leave town and drove off as fast as possible. To have exposed my wife to the strain of the journey and that of a household in mourning would have meant the loss of the baby.

It was afternoon when I arrived in the village. The heat was stifling and there was no one about in the streets. The dead man seemed to fill the tiny house. There was a smell of tears and priests. My mother, who suddenly looked like a little old lady of eighty, embraced me and held my head against her breast as if cuddling a tiny baby. There were very few relatives present: what with death and emigration, there weren't many left. My sister arrived the following morning and I hardly recognized her. A peach had turned into a dried fig. Her husband hadn't been able to come with her because at the factory where he worked the death of a father-in-law didn't qualify for such a long compassionate leave.

I took care of all the things that have to be done on such occasions, but there was no ostentation. It was a simple, dignified affair. And a fine coffin of dark wood.

By the evening of the second day my father was already underground. I could hardly believe it.

Everyone who came round to pay their respects kept asking 'But how did it happen?' He had fallen from the mule and knocked himself out. They had taken him to hospital and he didn't seem to be badly hurt; yet he was dead by midnight. The mule had run away and it had taken two days to find her. A fatal accident of the kind that was already regarded as something out of the ordinary because no one used animals any more: they all went out to the fields on their Vespas, mechanical diggers or tractors.

'He died for clinging to the old ways,' said the priest, a man I had known for years.

My sister went straight back to Grugliasco. I stayed a bit longer, but I was worried about my wife and went to the public phone every evening to ring her. The second evening there was no reply. The operator told me there was no fault on the line, so I went on trying that damned number until the exchange closed down, racking my brains trying to think what might have happened. I left early the next morning. My mother struggled to hold back the tears and blessed me and kissed my head over and over again.

There was no one at home. The place was in chaos, the bed unmade and things strewn all over the floor. But the door hadn't been forced, I had found it locked in the normal way. I threw myself at the telephone like a dog on a bone. Cosentino's wife told me he was out and she didn't know where he was, but as soon as I told her who I was and what had happened she began to cry.

'Haven't you heard what's been happening? Those bastards . . .'

The journalists, who always have to attach labels to

everything, had called it the night of the handcuffs. A dragnet had been thrown not only over Palermo, but over the whole of Italy in an operation planned with the utmost secrecy. Big fish and small fish, they raked in all they found.

A neighbour told me that when they came to the flat Nuccia had been taken ill. She was now in hospital and her sister was with her. I was certain they would arrest me if I went there, but not even the thought of losing my liberty could stop me. By tipping left, right and centre I managed to get through easily enough, mixing with the doctors and nurses. There were some guards posted here and there, but no *carabinieri* in the ward where my wife was.

She looked like death. She couldn't speak, and the doctor warned against trying to make her talk.

Before going, I took my sister–in–law out into the corridor and asked her what had happened. She was an idiot who couldn't even string two words together to make sense, and she was still in shock, but between sobs she told me that they had entered the flat by opening the door with a tool while she and Nuccia were asleep. They were carrying automatic rifles and pistols. They pulled them from their beds and threw everything all over the place. Nothing would convince them that I was not in the house at two o'clock in the morning. Nuccia wouldn't tell them where I was so they slapped her about. She collapsed. Then they shouted questions and insults at her to frighten her, and the marshal kneed her, causing her to fall again. Eventually they realized it was futile and went away.

Nuccia was already starting to lose blood, but her sister didn't notice this for a while and what with one thing and another a whole hour went by. If a neighbour hadn't phoned the Red Cross, that idiot of her sister would have let her die like that, lying on the floor. The doctor who examined her had said she was in a bad way but improving; there was nothing he could do to save the baby.

Cosentino had told me about two hideouts, one in the countryside, the other in town. I didn't know if they were still safe or not, but I cautiously tried the one in town, a new apartment in Viale della Regione. Two of my friends were there, both hiding from the police. We spent the afternoon and evening discussing what had happened and exchanging news. It was like a report from the front in time of war. Afterwards I slipped out to do some shopping and buy a paper. It was all there: names, addresses and everything. In Palermo the raids had been organized by Colonel Giuseppe Russo. I read the news out loud because my two friends had had little or no schooling.

The following night I returned to the hospital, not having dared to go again during normal visiting hours. Pocketing another tip, the nurse in charge took me to the ward. But Nuccia had apparently been discharged already, for in her place there was an old lady sleeping with her mouth open. This was a relief, the only problem being that it was too dangerous to go home and phoning was absolutely out of the question. So I went back to my hideout to do some hard thinking. I was desperate to see the poor girl again. I was through with lies. I had to tell her the truth and I wanted to choose the words very carefully.

During the afternoon a thought occurred to me. There was a butcher's shop only a few doors away from where I lived run by an old woman, a widow called Za Luigina, nicknamed 'a catanisa because she came from Catania. She was a good-hearted soul. I had done her a little favour once when her youngest son got into a spot of bother and now she made a great fuss of me whenever she saw me. I kept my eyes open on the way to the shop. One of our chaps who had a newspaper kiosk had told me that everything seemed to be quiet enough, but there was likely to be some action later in the evening. As soon as I got to the shop I signalled to Za Luigina that I wanted a word with her and she immediately led me into the office behind the shop.

'I need your help,' I told her. I wanted her just to tell my wife I was safe, and to ask if there was anything she needed.

'Shall I take her a little piece of meat?' asked Za Luigina, and cut off two nice slices of veal with her own hands. She wrapped them in the yellow paper that butchers always used in those days, and left. Her son was standing at the counter, and while he got on with preparing the mince, I waited in the office to avoid being seen by any customer who might come in. And while I waited I thought about how I could get in touch with the others without putting anybody at risk. Cosentino's wife hadn't told me, when I spoke to her on the phone, if he had been arrested or not. I should have to use a contact in the police to find out who was in and who was out.

When Za Luigina got back, there was a whole crowd of customers in the shop and I expected her to stay at the counter and give her son a hand for a few minutes. But she came straight into the office and shut the door. A large woman and no longer young, she had been hurrying and needed a moment to get her breath back. She stood with one hand clutching her heart while she wiped the sweat from her forehead with the other. I'll never forget the way she was looking at me.

'*Mossi!* – She's dead!'

Nuccia had died in hospital of a haemorrhage. That was why her bed had been given to another patient, not because she had been discharged. Za Luigina prattled on, holding me by the arm and saying 'Poor girl, poor girl!' and other things. The poor old lady had tears in her eyes. I wasn't listening. I loosened the gun in the holster and left.

First I went home. The relatives were already there, all women apart from one, the new husband of one of Nuccia's sisters, a *mulu fausu*[2] who lived off the earnings of his dressmaker wife. Also there was the aunt who had got Nuccia her job in the restaurant where I had met her.

'Be careful, Giovanni: they've already been here twice looking for you,' she said while the others were embracing me and saying all the usual empty words. She was the only real person in that gaggle of geese. I took her to one side and gave her some money. I couldn't go to the mortuary myself and she would have to make all the arrangements. I told her that I felt Nuccia should be buried in her own village in the same cemetery as her parents.

'Don't worry, I'll take care of it.'

'No one must touch any of her things here, and I want everyone out as soon as possible.'

'Don't worry.'

She was a strong woman, a woman of character. It was under her supervision that Nuccia and I had begun our courtship. I remember how she used to watch me to make sure I wasn't simply fooling about like all the other customers, but had honourable intentions. She had been genuinely fond of her niece, and of all Nuccia's relatives she is the only one I keep in touch with.

I returned to the hideout. There was a message waiting for me from Cosentino: I was to be outside the church of San Giovanni degli Eremiti at ten o'clock that evening. My friends had heard the news from him and embraced me. They didn't know what else they could do, but had there been anything I needed they would have gone even into the police station to get it. When I told them there was nothing I needed, they left me in peace to shave. I heard them speaking in low voices and then closing the door softly to avoid disturbing me.

It was eight o'clock in the evening. I got into my car and wedged my gun between the two front seats. If they stopped me I had no intention of escaping. I drove to the quayside at Sant'Erasmo and sat on one of those iron things they use for tying up fishing boats. It was still light and the last fishermen were putting away their rods and pails. I looked at the still, dirty water and thought about my life. In no time at all I had lost father, wife and child. Only my mother was left, and then I should be living only to eat and sleep. If I threw myself into the water I would go down like a stone: just time to say Christ help me and my misery would be over. Then I remembered those who had come looking for me with guns, ready to shoot me. I remembered the policemen who had knocked me about and those who had knocked my wife about. Why should I die just to please them?

Cosentino arrived punctually at ten in a car belonging to a certain Greco who was friendly with both him and Teresi. He got out of the car and, without a word, hugged me with all his strength. I remember that still. Then he pushed me into the car and we drove out of town. As we went he told me how they had arrested him and released him almost at once, as they had done with many others. But Mimmo Teresi was still in prison. I was still in danger because a grass had mentioned my name in a statement. Until I was fixed up with a lawyer I had to lie low.

'So in the meantime you're staying with me.'

He took me to a house in the country occupied by his family. They all greeted me in a very kind and courteous way and his wife asked after Nuccia. When

129

she heard about her death and that she had been pregnant at the time, she said 'Poor girl, poor girl!' like Za Luigina. They forced me to eat a plateful of *parmigiana di melanzane* and something else as well. I was given a bedroom to myself. Cosentino left early in the morning and returned at two o'clock in the afternoon.

From just after lunch until late in the evening, people came and went and there was much exchanging of news. Everything had ground to a halt; the police were still making arrests and no business could be done. In exchange for hospitality I did some gardening: there was a lemon orchard, a small kitchen garden and some trees both for fruit and shade. I raked, pruned, dug in fertilizer and kept myself too busy to think about sad things.

I can't remember if Stefano and his father were arrested then or later when I was staying with my mother. Don Paolino was in hospital in Naples and his son was looking after him. But I knew the solidarity of the Family. The arrest changed nothing because Stefano continued to give the orders from his cell. They explained that a regent is only nominated if the *capo* dies, otherwise things go on just as before.

I stayed with Cosentino for nearly a week, and they only let me go when I explained that my mother was on her own and knew nothing yet of my wife's death. I had to tell her myself.

'Are you short of cash?' Cosentino asked. The purchase of the land, the wedding and two funerals had left me flat broke, but I knew that the Family had its problems with so many members in prison: nothing was coming in and vast sums were being spent on lawyers and help both for the men in prison and their relatives outside.

'I'm all right, there's nothing I need.'

'As soon as you get there, find out whether anyone's been looking for you.'

'Don't worry, I will,' I assured him. He sent me off with a jokey phrase that one heard from time to time in those days:

'*Acqua davanti e ventu darreri* . . . '[3]

Even after all these years I have never been able to repay his generosity, and this is my one regret.

Notes

1. Now the innocent will pay for the guilty.
2. A sluggard, a sponge.
3. Literally: 'The sea ahead and a following wind.'

XII

At home I found a little old woman who no longer did any cooking but spent her time either sitting outside the door or mending things of my father's that were no use to anyone. There was nothing wrong with my mother's brain, but all her energy had gone. Sometimes she would be sitting in her chair with her eyes shut and it was impossible to tell if she was asleep or just thinking about something. I knew she felt how I had felt that evening on the quay: alone and with no reason to go on living.

I kept asking her questions to make her talk because she enjoyed talking. And to give her something to do I pretended to need looking after like any other man: trousers to be ironed, shirts to be mended, meals to be cooked. And she did her best. She no longer asked me if I was stopping, knowing that I would have to leave, that my life was elsewhere. We also talked about the land. As I couldn't see to it myself, it would have to be either sold or rented out to someone we could trust. I asked if the owners of the neighbouring land had been to make an offer. After waiting so long, surely they wouldn't let the chance slip now?

'No one has called here,' said my mother, and changed the subject. Thinking that it hurt her to consider selling the land that had made her husband so happy when I bought it, I decided not to raise that particular subject again. I had no other worries. The police hadn't come

132

looking for me; they obviously had more important things to do in Palermo.

I went to our holding every day. My father had had time to do some work on it before his death, and the crops had been harvested. Before burning the stubble I wanted to discuss it with the neighbours; if they were willing, we could do it together and then maybe hire a tractor to plough both plots, thus reducing the costs. But they were never on their holding and I never saw them in the village.

The night before I left it was so hot I couldn't rest. I kept tossing and turning and thoughts were whirling about in my head, when suddenly a thought struck me quite unexpectedly and I sat bolt upright in bed. I peered at my mother to see if she was awake.

'*Mamà* . . . '

She was. I went to sit on the edge of her bed. Why was it that the neighbours still hadn't made an offer for the holding? And why was it that they were never there when I was? And why was it that they hadn't even come to my father's funeral nor to pay their respects?

'Go to sleep, Giovannino. It's late,' my mother replied, turning over. Then I knew I was right.

'You must tell me how my father died,' I said quietly. But I wasn't expecting so much pain. She wept, repeating over and over again that after losing her husband and pregnant daughter–in–law, she was now about to lose her son as well. And she begged her Creator to let her die and be reunited with that blessed soul in heaven. At last I realized that the cause of her despair was my gun and what I might do with it. She told me that my father had sworn her to silence from his hospital bed.

He had not fallen from the mule. He had been beaten up by the neighbours out of envy and sheer spite. They had set about an old man simply because they were angry at being thwarted. They had probably not meant to kill him, and when they realized what they had done they were too terrified even to turn up at the funeral, not knowing what my father had said before he died. And as soon as they heard I was in the village, they had dropped out of sight.

It took me most of the night to comfort my poor old mother and calm her down. I swore on the memory of my wife and my unborn child that I would never cause her the grief of seeing me sent to prison on account of those vile, despicable people. She slept at last, and I spent the rest of the night thinking about my father. His dying thought had been for my safety. He didn't want revenge, he didn't, maybe, even want me to know how he met his end. It is not dignified for an old person to die as he had died.

I say no more. If people understand these things, words are unnecessary. If they don't understand, then not all the words that have ever been written would be enough.

The atmosphere in Palermo was one of gloom and doom. The Ucciardone prison was full and dozens of people had been sent on prolonged trips to the mainland. Di Cristina was among those in prison. I hadn't seen him for a long time.

Liggio, Riina, Provenzano and nearly all the Corleone *cosca* were at liberty, fugitives only in a sense, because everyone knew that Liggio had acquired a sudden taste for *panettone milanese* and a friend of mine said he had seen Riina at Partinico. Provenzano spent part of his time in Sicily and part in Rome.

The atmosphere in my flat was even worse, however. To come home in the evening and find the place in darkness, no smell of cooking coming from the kitchen and an empty bed, was more than I could bear. I cleared everything out and left. Although I no longer needed to worry about my wife, I didn't like the idea that a group of uniformed villains could barge into my home whenever they felt like it and cart me off to the *questura* or the police station to give me a going over at their leisure. I informed Cosentino that I wanted a freer life-style, living in a bed and breakfast or with friends or in one of our safe houses, whatever came along.

This would have been unthinkable ten years earlier, but things had changed in the Families rather like they do in the army: the rules were the same but the discipline was no longer there. The new *picciotti* stood around with their hands in their pockets and insolence written all over them; they thought themselves superior to Turi Giuliano and when they replied to a question didn't even bother to take the cigarette out of their mouths.

My own legal situation had righted itself. The lawyer who had been briefed on my behalf returned to say that the case against me had been dropped because of the absence of a *corpus delicti*. He explained what this meant: they couldn't find a body. He hadn't even been able to find out the name of the dead man they were looking for. Cosentino, who was experienced in these matters, explained the situation to me.

'No one's grassed, as such. Someone already in prison has made a statement with the proviso that he isn't named. The authorities have tried to act on the information but have run up against a brick wall. As they know that you will never confess voluntarily, their only hope is to find a body, but until they do nobody can say that this person is dead. Do you understand?'

This made it difficult to find out who had been singing and what incident he was referring to. Cosentino said he would made some enquiries, but these were difficult times and there were more important things to be done. The city was changing, people were changing, the mentality was changing. Money was coming in, real money. Construction deals used to take years what with arranging licences, sites, labourers, finance and so on. Now one swift requisition netted thousands with no problem. And that was still peanuts. Drugs were just starting to appear. Some people were already dealing in them, others had no idea what they were, and everybody called them something different. But I'll come back to that later.

One evening I heard someone call my name as I walked along the street. It had occurred to me that I hadn't had a pizza in ages, and I fancied one. I turned. It was Tano's girl. I had forgotten all about her, but she hadn't changed at all. She said Tano still hadn't reappeared and she thought he must have gone to the States to avoid trouble of some kind. Many had done the same.

I took her to a pizzeria near the Politeama. She was working as a sales girl in a perfumery now. She said she hardly thought about Tano any more. If he had left the country, he must have had a good reason for it. While we were eating I remembered her name: Lucia. I asked her if she had a boyfriend.

'No ties.'

She lived in an ancient palazzo in Vicolo Castelnuovo. We went up a very long, narrow, winding staircase past open landings and narrow passages. At the top was a small room with a tiny terrace; the view was of more old palazzi and churches I had never seen before. Lucia lived alone, and I wondered why, seeing she had parents and brothers and sisters. She was a strange girl and never spoke about herself. As I told Cosentino, if she had been a man she would have made a good operator.

Meanwhile, work had picked up. I was thinking of extending the house in the village by adding a second storey with two extra rooms. Everyone at the time was building with prefabricated sections, and in some cases, where only a few years before there had been one-storey *bassi*, there now stood villas with polished wooden shutters. Modernizing one's home and putting in a ceramic bath and papered walls was all the rage; no one would bat an eyelid if they saw builders working on our house too.

It made my mother happy as well, imagining that I was enlarging the house ready for when I should re–marry and return to the village for good. In fact, although I had got over my wife's death by this time, I knew I should never re–marry. But how could I say this to a poor old woman who had no one but me in the world? To keep her busy I had the work done in dribs and drabs so she was always having to cope with carpenters, plumbers and plasterers and had no time to think about other things.

Stefano had been released by now. To celebrate this, there had been a feast of *pasta al forno* and meat roasted over the fire in his house in the country. I missed this, as I was in hospital with a bullet in my leg. This was my only injury in thirty years, but I had been taken so completely off my guard that it was a wonder I wasn't killed.

This is how it happened. I was living at the time in a nice flat belonging to a friend who was in prison in the north of Italy. He had entrusted me with the keys and told me to look after everything. Tired of furnished rooms and prying landladies, I had decided to move in for six months at least. Lucia went on living in her own flat, but I asked her round from time to time. She cooked the things I liked and was really splendid. We watched some television and then slept together. There's nothing like having a woman in one's bed. When times were difficult

I would make do with a prostitute and still enjoy it. It's the company I like. Maybe I had spent too many nights in the mule's manger, or sharing a bed with my brothers, or with mice. Or even quite alone, which is the worst thing in the world.

One evening Totuccio Federico arrived. He had an air of mystery about him which I knew spelled work. While Lucia washed the dishes in the kitchen, he explained that there was something that needed straightening out. A certain mechanic called Lo Presti had started messing with contraband goods on his own account and contrary to the rules. When he was given his first warning he pulled a gun. There was no way he would listen to reason.

We worked out all the details. Totuccio asked if I wanted help, but I refused: I knew my job by this time and preferred to work alone. I had to invent an excuse for Lucia because I had promised to take her to the cinema the following evening.

Lo Presti had a small workshop in a street that isn't there any more, an area of decaying buildings, dirt, damp and unending rows of shops. In the afternoon I collected an *innocente* from the usual garage and drove up to the sanctuary on top of Monte Pellegrino. The car was a Fiat 127 with only about a thousand kilometres on the clock, and it was such a pleasure to drive that I decided there and then to buy one.

Federico had given me a detailed description of the mechanic and I recognized him as soon as he appeared outside the workshop door. He looked a bit like Michele Cavataio, but much younger: he can only have been about twenty–two at the most, short and broad–shouldered. He was wiping his hands on a piece of rag and talking to a *pilu russu*.[1] He looked anxious. 'He's seen the writing on the wall, poor kid,' I thought as I watched him, well hidden in my 127. As soon as the *pilu russu* went off, I got out of the car. The mechanic was still wiping his hands on the rag. He glanced at me and disappeared into the workshop. I strolled casually towards the door with my hands in my pockets and eyes on the ground. Before going in I glanced up and down the street. There was a group of children playing with a football down one end and a little old man sitting in front of his house smoking a cigar, the usual *mezzo toscano*. Not a car in sight. The conditions were perfect. But when I peered through the door into that dark hole stinking with oil, there was no sign of Lo Presti. Instead, there were two armed men who fired so quickly that I didn't have time to draw my gun.

I didn't even notice I'd been hit. I turned and ran, but realized that if I tried to get into the car those two would catch up with me and I should be dead meat. Luckily at that very moment a small open truck was passing by loaded with boxes of fruit. Hearing the shots, the driver had speeded up to get out of the way. As soon as he was level with me, I leapt on to the tailboard. The gunmen started firing again, but as soon as they saw I had a gun in my hand, they threw themselves to the ground. Not that I could have even taken a pot shot at them because at that moment the pain really hit me.

The truck was speeding along now. The poor wretched driver kept turning round and peering at me through the little window behind his seat. His eyes were like saucers and his mouth hung open. He didn't know what to do. He kept going but I was going with him. Eventually he braked, leapt out and took to his heels. I did the same, gritting my teeth, trying not to think of the pain. I sped down a couple of side streets and was out of trouble. But I was leaving a trail of blood. I found a telephone and called Federico, who was waiting for a report. I told him where to pick me up.

After I'd spoken to him it struck me that I'd suggested a place much too far away. I thought I'd never get there without help in the state I was in. But I set off. As I went, quite a few people passing by noticed the blood streaming from the wound and turned round to stare. But although I'd never had much time for the natives of Palermo, I have to admit that they know how to mind their own business. No one said a word. The car was waiting when I got there. Federico was in it, but the driver was a mere stripling of a *picciotto* I had never set eyes on before, and he drove like a maniac.

'What happened?' asked Totuccio. I tried to explain, but I wasn't thinking clearly after losing all that blood. I was semiconscious by the time we reached *'u spitaleddu*. I heard the doctor say:

'We'll have to put him under.'

After the operation I was in bed for two weeks. That was why I missed the party for Stefano Bontate.

The *spitaleddu* was no luxury clinic. I only saw the doctor for a couple of minutes morning and evening; his wife saw to my basic necessities and for the rest of the time I was alone. During the night I slept like a log, during the day I gazed at the ceiling and thought. As soon as my strength returned I began to have visitors. The first to come was Cosentino. He was slightly the worse for wear himself, having smashed into a van and got a cut on his forehead.

'How are you feeling, Giovannino?'

'Better.'

'Rather you than me,' he said jokingly. This expression, '*Abbonè chi capitàu a tia*', was one we used in my village, too, and it made me laugh. He delivered good wishes from his family, our friends and Stefano himself. We discussed the shooting incident. I told him that I didn't understand how on earth those friends of the mechanic's had found out I was going there to get him. Cosentino interrupted me.

'Not friends. Police.'

That took my breath away. Not because of the way they had gone for me. There were plain-clothes policeman in circulation now who were so obviously villains that one was tempted to cross the road to avoid them; and over–exposure to American gangster films had taught them to shoot first and ask questions later. No, the real question was: who had warned them? The only explanation possible was that Lo Presti had a secret deal with the authorities. So he himself had called for help as soon as he realized he was in danger.

'A double traitor,' said Cosentino.

'As soon as I'm on my feet I'll sort him out.'

'You're not going to sort anyone out. You've got to get better. That sonofabitch will get what's coming to him, don't worry. But you're going to take a holiday.'

My holiday was a week in Rome acting as bodyguard to a friend of the Bontate family. Bodyguards came in two categories, and the first thing you had to ask a customer – half in jest and half for real – was if he wanted a guard '*di cumparsa o di sustanza?*'[2] The first kind is only to impress, to keep people at a distance even if the bulge under the armpit is nothing more lethal than a ham roll. A bodyguard *di sustanza*, on the other hand, has to know how to shoot straight and must be absolutely trustworthy.

Stefano's friend was Nino Salvo.[3] I had never seen him before and didn't know anything about him. He struck me as a *gran signore* and from the way he treated me I realized he had no experience in dealing with people from my sort of background. We travelled by sleeping car and he had plenty of time to explain what he wanted me to do when he met the people who were expecting him. I was always to stay three steps behind him, when he went into a room I was to stand by the door like a member of the Swiss guard, and at restaurants I was to sit at a nearby table and, after the meal deal with the bill. Theatricals were a new departure for me, but it made a pleasant break coming after so much that had been anything but pleasant, and when we parted *Signor* Salvo praised me for doing a good job.

I had been chosen because I was presentable and had a clean record. When we arrived in Rome he took on a secretary as well, a girl with red hair who was an absolute knockout. She was, of course, a secretary *di cumparsa*, and he took her with him wherever he went. What with me and his secretary, I think he cut quite a figure with his colleagues in Rome. When his guests looked at me and tried to appear unconcerned it made me want to laugh, and I'm sure that if I'd said 'boo' to any of them they'd have run away with their tails between their legs.

We talked for a while at the hotel in the evening. He was curious and asked a lot of questions, but as soon as he realized I preferred not to answer them, he stopped. On the third evening he took the red–headed secretary to his room and that was the end of our chats. The following morning he told me to hire a taxi and go and see the sights without worrying about the cost. It was a sunny day and there was plenty to see. Rome was bigger and more beautiful than Palermo and there were fewer signs of poverty, but I missed the sea.

I enjoyed my day out. When I got back, Signor Salvo was looking pleased with himself; he'd evidently got the deal sewn up. He wanted to give me a present, and as I had no orders to the contrary, I accepted. I had handled quite a lot of money in my life, but until that moment I had never received a cheque for my work. And it was a good fat cheque. As we parted he said:

'Thanks for all you've done, Giovanni. And all the best.'

I thought how lucky I was to have met him. But I could hardly know at that stage that my acquaintance with him was to save my life.

Notes

1. Man with red hair.
2. 'For show or for real'.
3. *Nino Salvo*. Until the early sixties, Nino and his cousin Ignazio managed the Sicilian tax offices and raked in sums of money far exceeding those collected in other regions of Italy. Friends of Bontate and the so–called 'declining' section of the Mafia, they also had connections in the highest political circles and all investigations into their activities failed until 1984, when they were arrested for associating with the Mafia. Nino died of cancer in Switzerland two years later. Ignazio is currently serving a seven–year sentence (with one year's remission).

XIII

There was a surprise waiting for me when I came out
of hospital: the 127 I had been planning to buy had
already been ordered and paid for and would be ready
for collection on Monday morning. It was a present from
the Family by way of compensation for the injury.

Friday afternoon was windy. I went to see a friend
who was interested in my Giulia and we settled the deal
at once. Then I went to the flat to see if everything was
all right. I had already heard that it was not being
watched so it was quite safe. I watered a plant in
the sitting room that looked as droopy as I felt and
then left straight away. I wanted good food and plenty
of it because at 'u spitaleddu, with the excuse that I was
more dead than alive, they had only given me thin soup
made with a cube and slivers of meat thin enough to be
transparent. And I wanted to see the sea.

Because Cosentino was out of town, I couldn't meet
him until Sunday morning. There were things he wanted
to say to me, but there were also things I wanted to say
to him. So we shut ourselves up in his living room for a
couple of hours, alone at first and then with some other
people. In the evening I had a good shower and then
went to see Lucia. She was getting ready to go out, and
as she was all dressed up I teased her by saying she had
got herself a new boyfriend before knowing if she was a
widow or not. She looked at me very tenderly and kept
stroking my face.

'So you're better now, are you? Where have you

been all this time? Couldn't you have let me know?'

'The fact that I didn't means that I couldn't.'

'Beast. There I was, looking for you in every hospital in town, and you turn up like this, complete with suit and aftershave.'

'Aren't you glad to see me?' I asked, laughing.

She swore she was and I said she was lying in her teeth and that, like St Thomas, if I couldn't get my hands on the proof I wouldn't believe her. So by the time we left the flat it was too late for a meal in any of the restaurants I knew and we had to make do with a couple of *arancini di riso*[1] and a pastry in a place that stayed open after midnight. We got back to her flat at about one. Lucia undressed immediately. I watched her in silence until she turned to me and said:

'What's up?'

'The moment's come when I have to tell you something . . . '

I told her all about the Tano business, the orders I had been given and what had happened that night in the hut. She listened standing there stark naked, her face as white as white. She asked me if he had suffered.

'Don't worry: he never knew what hit him.'

'Where is he now?'

'God knows. Maybe at the bottom of an abandoned well, or . . . '

I had never heard a woman use foul language, not even in the village. She scratched my neck and when I tried to push her away she bit my hands. She yelled and spat. I couldn't stop her attacking me and at one point, in self defence, I had to punch her in the stomach. 'I knew it, you stinking bastard! I knew it all along!' she screeched. And then she moaned: 'My poor darling! My poor baby!', weeping so much and with such evident grief

145

that poor Tano would have felt extremely flattered if he could have heard her.

When she saw that scratching and kicking were getting her nowhere, she decided to use a knife on me, but I barred her way to the kitchen, grabbed her and threw her on to the bed. I explained that if the same orders had been given to Tano, it would have been him who shot me.

'I wish he had!' she screamed. At last she quietened down and lay curled up like a dog with her mouth pressed into the sheet, whispering something I couldn't hear. She didn't raise her head when I went out. I left the door on the latch and set off down the long, long, narrow staircase. I thought about Tano. He had been a conceited fop who thought of nothing but smart clothes and combing his hair every five minutes, and his punishment made it clear that he had not known how a *uomo d'onore* should behave. Yet Lucia had loved him quite as much as Nuccia had loved me. Women are like that. They don't judge, they accept or refuse, and when they accept they accept one hundred per cent.

The little courtyard at the bottom of the staircase was in darkness. I stopped and two figures stepped out from behind an archway. One was Emanuele D'Agostino, the other was the youngster who had driven me to the doctor after the shooting; I later learned his name was Carmelo and his friends called him Melo or Muluzzo. D'Agostino said nothing; he lifted his head with a gesture that meant: well?

'Go on up. The door's on the latch.'

'OK.'

'Goodnight,' I said, raising a hand in farewell, and walked off with my hands in my pockets and my eyes on the ground.

No one but Lucia could have told the police about the proposed visit to Lo Presti. She had heard us talking the night that Totuccio Federico came to give me the instructions. It was the opportunity she had been waiting for all this time. She had come looking for me at the Eden bar hoping that I would tell her what I knew. When I didn't, she decided to become my woman, swearing that she no longer cared about Tano, that his walking out on her without even bothering to tell her what was happening had made her angry and bitter.

'So you're better now, are you?' she had asked when I turned up at her flat. If I hadn't already smelled a rat, I should have asked her what I was supposed to be better *from*. Most people only knew that I had disappeared. No one could have told her more than that except the policeman who shot me and saw my blood on the road. And the reason they had told her was because Tano's girl was an informer.

I had discussed it with Cosentino, but I had to be absolutely sure of the facts before making the final decision. That was why I had confessed the Tano business to her. Her reaction had swept away any remaining doubts. It was not the first time that I had looked into the eyes of someone who wanted to kill me. Love can be hidden. Not hate.

This was what D'Agostino and Carmelo had been waiting for: to know if they were to go up to the flat or not. I had said yes. So goodbye Lucia.

One of the things that happened at about the same time was what the press called 'the Leonardo Vitale affair'. They made a fuss about it because there was nothing else to fill the front pages with banner headlines and big photographs, no news to make everyone gasp: *'Bedda matri!*: Blessed Madonna!' They mourned the passing of the (to them) golden age of Ciaculli and Vitale Lazio. Vitale was a slightly unbalanced type who had decided to shop his friends and tell all. They were calling him *'Il primo pentito*, the first penitent'.

I knew him very well. I had met him at the Cuba bar. In a couple of words he had established that we were of the same Family, and then there had been no stopping him. He read me a sermon that wouldn't have shamed a priest on Good Friday. I listened open-mouthed. At first I was amused, because he had a way of speaking that I can't describe, a patchwork of Italian, local dialect and *baccagghiu*[2] that at times was impossible to follow. Then I began to get worried, because he was really letting loose and saying things that could have been incriminating. Eventually, I became convinced that he was mad, and the same day I told Cosentino about him. But he had problems of his own and before I had finished started shouting:

'Cui, ddu foddi? Ddu scimunitu!'[3]

The next time I met Vitale he was so chummy that anybody who saw us could have been forgiven for thinking that we had been nursed at the same breast. And I had guessed that he was jealous. He had it in especially for Curiano.[4] He had heard people referring to him and *Scarpuzzedda*[5] as the two best *uomini d'onore* in Palermo and was green with envy. *Scarpuzzedda*, however, was unpopular. I knew him, but had heard people complain that he was curt, the type of man who wouldn't put himself out for anyone. Curiano, on the other hand, had a splendid reputation and everyone admired him. This made Vitale see red.

Because he had once been a choirboy and had a relative in the church, he had set himself up as a preacher and pretended to speak on behalf of God Almighty – who didn't know him from Adam. And because no one would take him seriously, he had ended up by unburdening his heart to the first police officer who was ready to listen.

This was fifteen years ago, remember. Not all that long but, still, things were different. No one thought for a moment that someone like Vitale would spill his guts, flying in the face of his oath as a *uomo d'onore*. That was why Cosentino took no notice when I warned him. Not even the police took Vitale seriously. When he spoke, everyone laughed. Killing him when he got out of prison years later was nothing but an empty gesture,[6] but the mentality of his killer was the new mentality, the only mentality that counts now: shoot first, think later, based on the assumption that dead men can't hurt you. First you kill the man, then you ask yourself what he might be going to do.

I forgot all about Vitale when Liggio was re-arrested in May '74 in a house in Milan. I had heard from Teresi, Stefano himself and various other people that he was hiding in Milan, but had never been sure if it was true or not. I was naïve enough to think that once Mangano had the handcuffs on him I should be safer. But Riina and Provenzano were still free then, in '74, and they still are to this day. I never understood how it was that Liggio ended up in gaol while his two lieutenants didn't. 'Some day I'll explain,' Mimmo Teresi, God rest his soul, said to me one evening. He was laughing.

Di Cristina was freed eventually. I tried to see him in Palermo, but something always prevented me, so when I had the chance I went to call on him in Riesi.

The door was opened by his wife, a handsome, dark-haired lady wearing glasses whom I had never seen before. He had aged slightly and looked tired, but he greeted me warmly and we drank a cup of coffee together.

'And how's the Falcon?'

He was referring to Stefano Bontate. This was, I knew, a name used by some of his friends. But what could I tell him? I wasn't in direct contact with Stefano; my *capo* was Cosentino. I took orders from him, from D'Agostino, Teresi and others. There was only one thing I could say: that Stefano was a good lad, straightforward, conscientious, a true *uomo d'onore*. My guiding principle had always been: never betray. And I had never betrayed a friend in my life. Apart from this, I had a special affection for Stefano that I had never had for anyone else. I would have risked my life for him had it ever been necessary. I explained this and Di Cristina told me he appreciated what I was saying.

'*Ogni stigghia au patruni assumigghia*.[7] I know you're loyal, Giovanni. And I know that everything you have said about Stefano is right. That's why he and I are such friends. But our day is drawing to a close . . . '

I asked him, with respect, what he meant by this. He explained that honour and loyalty were things of the past and that anybody who didn't realize this was a fool or tired of living. When money entered into the equation other values went out of the window, and when really big money was concerned there was no room for anything else at all.

'Stefano and I are both university graduates, did you know that?'

'*Voscenza sì.*'

'That's our problem: we studied too much. The lion kills the buffalo because he is ignorant. Educate a lion and he becomes worthless, a prey to the jackals. Do you understand what I am saying?'

'*Voscenza no.*'

'Because the jackal is ignorant, he despises books. My father and Stefano's father sent us to university because they wanted us to be better than they had been. They were wrong, Giovannino; they couldn't have done us a worse service. I realized this. I don't know whether Stefano has.'

This was a long time ago and I can't remember exactly what was said. This, however, was the gist of the conversation. It was evening, we were alone together and his words made a great impression on me, an impression that has lasted. How could I forget? The tragic events that occurred later served to engrave them on my memory even more vividly. In the event, everything that was said that evening in Riesi was confirmed.

Before I left he entrusted me with several secret commissions that I was to carry out on his behalf in Palermo and Trapani. And he gave me a large sum of money, so much that I was embarrassed and didn't know what to say.

'Put it on one side. Before the month's out there will be some wonderful opportunities and you'll be able to use all the cash you can get your hands on. With a little capital and a little luck you could be a rich man.'

Even this did not cheer me up. He had me worried. If he was right, we were all in for stormy weather. For the first time the thought of retiring occurred to me. I knew it wasn't allowed, and I didn't want to do it, but if the Family was to be destroyed like the Doctor's I didn't want to look for another master. I was only forty–two, but I was beginning to feel old, and old people have a right to retire.

Pondering on these gloomy thoughts, I got to Palermo when it was already getting dark, and because I hadn't turned the lights on I was stopped by a motor–cycle patrol and given the first ticket of my life. It was on a green slip of paper and I've kept it ever since like a lucky charm. God knows why.

Notes

1. Rice balls coloured with saffron.
2. Mafia slang.
3. What, that idiot? That halfwit?

4. Coriolano della Floresta, a nickname for Totuccio Contorno.
5. Nickname for Pino Greco, one of the Ciaculli Family's gunmen.
6. He was killed on 2 December, 1984, six months after his release.
7. A tool is shaped by the hand that uses it.

XIV

God took my mother too. But this time he at least allowed me the consolation of being with her at the end. She was ill for nearly a year and eventually only left her bed to answer the calls of nature. I went to see her every week, and once or twice when I wasn't supposed to leave Palermo I made a secret dash, starting in the late afternoon, getting home, sleeping for a couple of hours and leaving again very early in the morning, at about five.

Her mind went two weeks before the end. She no longer recognized me. One evening I went to sit beside her as soon as I arrived and asked her how she felt and if there was anything I could get her. She answered *'Bene, grazie'* and *'Niente, grazie'* in a whisper that was almost too faint to hear, and when I got up to go to the toilet I heard her ask a neighbour who was sitting on the other side of the bed: *'Ma cu è chissu?'*[1]

The improvements had been very successful: there were two bedrooms and a bathroom in the new upper storey. But my mother had never wanted to go upstairs and continued to sleep on the ground floor, even though it was damp. She said that was what she was used to and she didn't want to use the new rooms because it would spoil them. But even the ground floor had been changed beyond recognition with quarry tiles on the floor and a fine glass chandelier. Who would have believed that the corner where the television stood now was the same place where the mule once ate, slept and answered the calls of nature? When that happened at night, in the dark, it used to make us children laugh, and my father sometimes made a joke about it, saying that it helped to keep us warm.

This time my sister's husband came with her. I hadn't seen my brother–in–law for many years, but he hadn't changed at all: a bit more shrivelled, but still the same spineless little rat with no sense of self–respect. He came to the funeral this time not out of any affection for his mother–in–law but because he wanted to get his hands as quickly as possible on what little inheritance there might be.

And, indeed, as soon as we got back from the cemetery he took me to one side saying that we should talk 'men's talk'.

'For myself, I never talk anything else,' I said, but subtleties such as this were lost on him. He took me by the arm and asked what I intended to do about the house and the smallholding. I told him that the house was no longer the cattle shed he remembered because with my own money I had bought, refurbished and extended it. And the land I had bought too, putting it in my father's name for legal reasons. I set everything out nice and clear even though I was aware that he knew it all just as well as I did.

'Still, I don't want to leave my sister empty–handed and I don't want her to have only the pittance she's entitled to,' I hastened to add, and did some quick sums there and then. Valuing everything in accordance with local going rates, and assuming for the purpose that both house and land had been bought with my parents' money, I offered him a good round lump sum, in cash. He lit a cigarette and said he would think about it for a moment.

'There's nothing to think about. It's all you're getting, take it or leave it.'

He lowered his eyes. I knew he would take it, that he had come because he was afraid he wouldn't get anything at all. But he was the kind of man who, if you offered him a billion, would try to squeeze out another hundred lira. They wanted to stay for two or three days, but I wanted to be alone and after twenty–four hours I couldn't have stood the sight of my brother–in–law even in a photograph. And as for his daughters, who were grown up by now, they hadn't even bothered to come and accompany either their grandfather's or their grandmother's coffin to the cemetery. Gina showed me their photographs: on the beach half–naked with one boyfriend, in the countryside with another, on the Po with a third. They had no work, they weren't married, they had no duties. Only rights. Just as well that an old–fashioned man like my father had only seen them once or twice and only when they were tiny.

Enough of that. I said there was urgent work waiting for me in Palermo and that I had to leave as soon as possible and shut up the house. My sister started to cry as we said goodbye.

'How are we ever going to see each other again now?' she asked, embracing me. She had become the type of woman who passes from smiles to tears in no time at all. I could imagine her crying over films on the television and all that kind of rubbish. But she was fond of me in her way. I told her that I should never forget her and I kept my word.

After they left I returned to the cemetery to say goodbye to my mother all alone. I had had a beautiful tombstone made, with oval black and white photographs, as the custom was years ago. My father was wearing his *coppola*[2] and his usual dark suit with a waistcoat, and my mother had her hair done up in a bun and her face was very peaceful. Side by side, as they had lived.

'Won't you be coming back again?' asked a cousin, older than me, who I never saw except at weddings and funerals. He wasn't worrying about the prospect of not being able to embrace me again, only fishing for information about the smallholding. Although stupid, he was an able and competent farmer, so we drew up an agreement giving him a three–year lease on the land.

My frequent visits to my mother had got me used to travelling backwards and forwards: I knew the road now like the back of my hand. But when I left the village early the following morning, it occurred to me that I would probably not be returning for another six months, perhaps even a year. And when I did, the door would no longer be opened at my knock. I should have to use the key. And it would be the first time in my life, because I had never before had the keys to that house.

Without my mother to think about, my head was clear. I had no worries. I could think about anything I wanted to now. And this was the time when the money started to flow. Real money, as Di Cristina had forecast.

Some people had been dealing in drugs for ten years already. They were the ones who had friends in the United States. They imported the stuff from God knows where, using the same system as for the cigarettes: ship, fishing boat, lorry. Then they re–exported it to America, and the money they pocketed was worth fifty consignments of cigarettes. Gradually more and more people got in on the act until eventually everyone had dipped his bread into that gravy.

As neither the money nor the packets of powder ever came anywhere near me, I once asked Cosentino why on earth the Family didn't get in on such a lucrative business. He explained that Stefano wasn't keen on this kind of merchandise, though he had left other people free to make their own decisions about it.

'I dabble in a small way myself, from time to time. Only by putting up the odd bit of cash, however. I don't get personally involved.'

The people who brought the stuff in were called 'the Turks'. They asked a certain price. The people who came along to buy it with American dollars were called 'the cousins', because they were nearly always Americans of Sicilian origin. They paid another price. The difference between the two was the profit. When local people were only acting as middlemen and organizing the transport, one million up front would net ten or fifteen million, depending on the quality. Then the chemists came in. I don't know where they learned the techniques, but they knew how to work the raw material brought in by 'the Turks' and produce refined stuff ready for sale on the streets. And another lot took over the responsibility for shipping, using oranges, furniture, coffins and anything else that was suitable.

And 'the cousins' started to pay a very different price. Before now, 'billion' was a word I had read in the papers; they used it when they wrote about state finances. Now I began to hear it on the lips of people who, five years earlier, counted the change from a thousand–lira note. It was like being in a *putìa di vinu*[3] as I remembered them from years ago in the village. When I dropped in late in the evening, it would be crowded, everyone talking loudly and no one listening. Some were worse than others, but no one had a clear head. Bemused by the wine in their brains and their bellies, everyone was ready to sing or brawl as the fancy took him.

This is what it was like in Palermo for nearly a decade, until I left. Everyone was drunk with money. There were laboratories at Bagheria, at Partinico, at

Isola delle Femmine and in many suburban areas of the city. They were not private concerns, each one either belonging to a certain Family or, being situated in its zone of influence, coming under its protection. And the people connected to them had never been seen in Palermo previously. Everyone had partners: in Naples, Calabria, Greece, America. They had made such a fuss about me coming from a nearby district, and now here they were working alongside people who came from much further away, knowing that they were not *uomini d'onore* so that, once their business was completed, there was nothing to stop them talking.

I had very little to do. I was annoyed with Stefano for keeping out of these deals and with Cosentino for going along with him, so I refrained from asking every other minute for jobs to do, and for their part they never sent for me. So at best I did the odd deal involving half a kilo, and always with the same friends. Quick and safe. The profit would see me through the next couple of months without my having to raise a finger. I saw several of the laboratories during this period. They were always in the open countryside and screened by trees because of the smell.

The people working there were weird, their faces completely strange to me. No one was concerned about anything except the white powder. No one ever looked at me to see who I was. They were more drugged than the people who injected the filthy stuff into their veins. D'Agostino told me that they could make forty or fifty kilos of heroin a week with nothing more than a little equipment and two small rooms. Billions. And everyone who walked through the door had the same hungry look about the eyes that I had seen when I worked for the Doctor and went to the Palazzo dei Normanni. That, too, was a place awash with billions. People came there looking for senators and favours, knowing that a single word could make them for life.

Sometimes I did an escort job with friends. We put the little packets in the boot of the car without attempting to hide them. The rule was that if you were stopped you fired at once. That was when I saw a machine–gun close to for the first time. Indeed, Carmelo, who was himself killed by a machine–gun some time later, offered to teach me how to use it one evening. He said it was better than a pistol. A lad of only twenty, he knew all about machine–guns and had more than two billion in thirty different bank accounts, because if there was more than twenty million in any one account, the bank had to inform the police and reveal the name of the account holder. By now that was all people could understand: machine–guns and masses of money.

Just as this bonanza was getting under way, they kidnapped Luigi Corleo. Nino Salvo had married his daughter. It was a serious business. I wouldn't expect anyone to realize what an outrage of this magnitude actually meant. I could see further than the end of my nose by now, and I'm not ashamed to admit that when I heard the news my knees turned to jelly.

'Matter of a day or two,' said Teresi to Cosentino when I was with them one evening. But Cosentino looked solemn.

'I reckon he's already had it.'

He was right, but none of us knew it yet. Meanwhile, the days went by and there was no news. Then Stefano himself told me that he wanted to entrust three or four reliable *picciotti* with the task of finding Corleo and the men who had abducted him. Stefano knew that he could ask me to drop my other interests for a prolonged period and I would do so gladly, whereas some would have grumbled about the money they were losing.

I'll explain more later, but he was too soft–hearted for his own good. Someone with a sterner sense of authority was needed in times like that. If any one of his friends or relations criticized him, he let them do it and never held it against them.

But I knew that he asked me to this because he liked and trusted me, and I was proud of it. Cosentino slipped me a wad of one–hundred–thousand–lira notes and gave me some advice. He said I should start at Trapani, where the Family had old friends going back to the times of Don Paolino.

I searched for Corleo for a whole year. I worked like a policeman: watching houses, interrogating, buying information. By day I did nothing else, by night I thought of nothing else. One Sunday morning, at Erice, I ran into Nino Salvo. He asked how things were going, but I could tell that he had nearly given up hope.

'*Voscenza*, try not to worry, something will turn up,' I said eventually. He clapped me on the shoulder.

'Stefano said that if you couldn't crack this one, no one could . . . Eh, Giovanni, we had more fun in Rome, do you remember?'

I knew how important this mission was for me. We knew that the Corleonesi were behind the affair, so had I pulled it off I should have gained enormous prestige within the Family. But I failed. It was one of the biggest disappointments of my life. We never even discovered where he had been hidden, and this was the surest proof that they had killed him immediately. It hadn't been a real kidnapping. The ransom money meant nothing to these men. Their only aim was to insult.

When I finally returned to Palermo, Cosentino gave me a warm welcome.

'Holidays over, are they?'

That was a true word spoken in jest. There were to be no more holidays. The war had not yet started, though everyone knew it was only a matter of months. But business in the meantime continued at a frenzied pace, my friends were buying up apartments like one buys pastries: a dozen at a time.

The final happy occasion that I remember of this period was a trip in a fishing boat. No business involved, just a trip pure and simple. I had never been on the sea before and it was something I wanted to do. I had had plenty of invitations because several of my friends had bought motor boats, but I was wary of going so far with people who didn't really know what they were doing, especially since I couldn't swim. But with fishermen it was different, and while they worked I helped them. Farmers and fishermen do much the same sort of work and have the same calluses on their hands.

The old man at the wheel reminded me of my father, except that instead of a *coppola* he wore a red wool beret that gave him a boyish look. He didn't say much, but I managed to get him to tell me a bit about himself all the same. He worked for a *cavaliere*, and it was the *cavaliere* who owned the boat and the nets, who provided the diesel fuel and any equipment that was necessary, and saw to the upkeep and servicing of the engine. The fisherman was paid not by the hour but by the weight of the catch. The old man wasn't complaining.

'As long as my health lasts I shall go to sea,' he said.

'And when it fails?'

'Then my children will look after me,' he replied.

He had four sons and three daughters, and he knew that all seven of them were ready to do their duty by him.

That's how it should be. I, on the other hand, had

left my home and my village, thinking that just because I sent a bit of money I could have a clear conscience. This was why my father died, because his family all deserted him and the people who hated him thought they could beat him to death without fear of reprisal. A young man depends upon his courage; an old man depends upon his sons.

By the time we disembarked my mind was made up: the hour of retribution had come. I had promised my mother not to grieve her in this way, but now that she was in her grave the promise was void and I was free. I had already lost too much time: I didn't want to lose any more.

I went and asked Cosentino's permission. He knew the story already and showed no surprise. He said I was doing my duty, that he would have a word with Stefano but was certain that he would have no objection. He gave me a new pistol, a 7.65 with the registration number filed off.

'Don't worry if you have to ditch it afterwards. OK?'

'*Voscenza sì.*'

I went in search of Giuseppe Di Cristina. My village was not far from his and there was a risk that some police officer might try to lay the blame for this killing at his door. I found him in Palermo, staying with Totuccio Inzerillo. He listened to me like a father. It was possible that it could cause problems for him and he said there were things he would like to check out. If I heard nothing from him over the next ten days, I could carry on.

'If you go ahead, will you need any assistance?'

'*Voscenza no.*'

Two weeks later I had still received no message from him, so at the beginning of December I packed my bag and headed out of town.

Notes

1. Who is that man?
2. *Coppola*: a low–crowned cap with a peak, worn by Sicilian peasants.
3. Tavern.

XV

Snow was falling when I arrived, something I loved and hadn't seen for years. When I was a child, my mother used to give us spiced wine mixed with snow. It made a kind of *granita* and we ate it with bread. But my mother wasn't there any more and there was no wine in the house or anything else. I bought a few supplies and exchanged greetings with the neighbours who came in when they saw the lights on. In the evening I went to see my cousin.

He was embarrassed because the harvest had been poor. I listened to him in silence and when he had finished, neither blamed or praised him. Having realized that his nervousness was making him talk more freely than usual, I gradually led the conversation round to our neighbouring smallholders. He told me that the sickly brother had died during the summer. He had escaped me, but it didn't matter: a weak character, he had been a mere tool in the hands of his brother. And his brother was very much alive and kicking.

I ran into him in the village next day. It was Sunday and the weather had cleared up. He made quite a fuss of me. By now he had put everything out of his mind that he didn't choose to remember and was sure that I knew nothing of what had happened. He insisted on my joining him for a drink. There was a bar very near, but he dragged me off to one further away which was run by someone he called a 'mate' of his. The boy behind the bar poured him a glass of wine without waiting to be asked, and he drank it in a single gulp without even a splutter. He was obviously in practice. I suspected that the barman had become his 'mate' simply by letting him drink on tick – which is the matiest thing out.

At last he put his glass down.

'And how are things with you, then?' he asked. I wanted to laugh. Was he really still trying to get his hands on *'u setti tùmmina*? That's what it sounded like, but I was wrong, because as soon as I told him that by the grace of God I was doing pretty well, far from looking disappointed he grabbed me by the arm and steered me outside. His wife had been very ill, then with his brother dying he had had all the expense of the funeral, and his brother had left him with debts and two small children to bring up.

"A pena e 'a pinazza . . . '[1]

He went on and on, but with God's help eventually got to the point: he was prepared to sell me his smallholding. He wasn't offering it to me for lack of other bidders. They were, apparently, queueing up outside his door early every morning to get their hands on that piece of stony ground where the youngest olive tree was older than Methuselah. But he was giving me first refusal out of neighbourliness and because of the abiding friendship between our two families.

'If the price is right I might think it over,' I said, acting cool.

While I got myself a bit of supper at home, I was thinking that the Almighty had really come down on my side as far as this business was concerned. The owner of the adjacent land was called Paolino, and since killing my father Paolino had learned to drink heavily, work less and spend money. The plan came to me in a flash of inspiration. There was no need to be secretive, on the contrary, we should be seen together as much as possible, arm in arm like childhood pals.

This was no problem; he stuck to me like a crab–louse. At least four times a day he came knocking at my door, and he took me out to show me his land, which was badly tended, and to sing its praises as if it had been a daughter he was trying to marry off. He bought me one coffee after another, and while I drank coffee he was mixing wine, aperitifs and liqueurs. Although he was always the first to order a drink, soon it was nearly always I who paid, because his 'mate' behind the bar declared in front of everyone that unless he saw the money 'on the mahogany', he wouldn't let him have so much as a liqueur chocolate.

On Saturday morning we went to sign the contract at the notary's office where, in the presence of witnesses, I handed over five hundred thousand lira in cash. There were tears of joy in his eyes. He even wanted to kiss me, the Judas, and everyone laughed, including the notary. Then he dragged me off to his house for a meal, and on the way started to throw his money about: two kilos of pork ribs, the best; bananas for the guest, top quality; a tray of pastries freshly baked that morning. He bought wine as well: two big bottles. But here quality didn't concern him, only quantity.

At about four o'clock I said I had to go and get ready to leave. He kissed me again. It had got to be a habit. I went home, said my farewells to the neighbours and packed my case. By eight the temperature was well below freezing and every door was shut. I parked the 127 in a place on the village outskirts where it would go unnoticed in the middle of lots of other cars already parked there for the night. At about eleven I concealed myself in a dark doorway beside the road that Paolino would have to take on his way home from the bar. I thought of him in there, his pockets stuffed with my money, bragging about having got the townie to pay his asking price while the owner of the bar, once more his mate now that he had money to spend, poured him ten glasses one after the other and charged him for twelve.

I shivered a little as I waited. After living beside the sea for ten years I wasn't used to temperatures this low any more. I hadn't even got any gloves, and my shoes were too light by half. Also, I was a shade uneasy: in Palermo, once I was three hundred kilometres away from my own door no one would recognize me; and if they did, they knew they were duty bound not to know me. In the village it was different, I had to be careful.

He came along at about midnight. But not alone. He and a man I didn't know were walking arm in arm, both drunk and talking nineteen to the dozen. Luckily, Paolino saw his friend home. They stood outside the door exchanging bullshit for a quarter of an hour, until a woman came out and hauled her husband indoors.

Paolino shouted 'Buonu notte!' at the closed door, had a good pee against the wall and turned homewards. He was walking fairly straight, but very slowly. He got to a place which would have suited me fine, but there was a lighted window near and I could hear voices. I waited until he had turned the corner, and then ran to catch him up. He turned round. He wasn't that drunk, and as soon as he saw who it was, he opened his arms and grinned.

'My dear old mate, fancy seeing you!'

For years I had been working out what I would say to him when the moment came. I had the words all ready, each more ferocious than the last. I wanted him to be terrified, to crap his soul out, to throw himself on his knees at my feet . . .

But I was an old hand by now. This wasn't a vendetta, it was the fulfilment of a vow, an act of respect towards my father. So there was nothing to say. I put the pistol to his heart and that was the end of Paolino.

Back in Palermo I got busy at once, and in no time at all there were witnesses ready to swear on their children's heads that I was in town before ten o'clock and that we had eaten *sfincione*[2] together. Before leaving him, I had also removed Paolino's wallet and wedding ring. Everyone knew that I had paid him a large sum of money only hours previously, and they would naturally jump to the conclusion that some villain had decided to have a merry Christmas at his expense.

In short, I had thought of everything. But nothing at all happened for more than a year. In the meantime I had concluded the deal with his widow and she had handed over all the papers relating to the smallholding. Now, with my father's parcel of land and Paolino's, I had nearly two *salme*,[3] roughly six hectares. I had friends in Palermo who owned fifty apartments apiece, but my two *salme* made me feel like a tycoon and I wouldn't have swapped them even for the Bontates' villa and gardens.

Fourteen months after the incident I was contacted by officers from the *caserma* in Piazza Verdi, near the Teatro Massimo. I had never been there before but I knew about it from hearsay. The building had once been a convent, the entrance was in a narrow alleyway near an old arch and people said it was creepy after dark. But I'm not the impressionable type and, anyway, it was broad daylight when I went there.

I took my lawyer with me just to be on the safe side, but the days of heavy–handed, moustachioed marshals were long gone and I was interviewed by a young university–educated lieutenant who talked like a curate, called me 'sir' and was extremely polite. He began by asking questions about my trip to the village just before the tragic incident, until the lawyer cut him short and demanded to know if I was to be charged with anything.

'For the moment we are trying to establish the facts because the inquiries are not yet complete,' said the curate, slightly ruffled. What's this, I thought, how can the lawyer take umbrage when the officer's being so polite?

'I am at your service,' I said. And I explained that Paolino's death had caused me endless inconvenience because I had had to wait for probate before finalizing the deal, and as there were children involved this had meant a court order, and the courts took for ever to reach a decision in this type of case.

'The fact of the matter is,' explained the lawyer as we left the building, 'that the police know exactly who you are, record or no record, and that mate of yours chose a right moment to get killed just when you happened to be in the village.'

He laughed. I asked him if he thought there was likely to be any comeback in the future.

'The first time they put you inside for criminal association you'll find yourself paying not only for this but also for things you haven't done. But until that happens they can scratch their navels.'

So I put it out of my mind.

I had no choice, anyway. The war was hotting up again and by this time I knew the scene well enough to realize that it was going to be a biggie.

It wasn't little men any longer who were being liquidated. At first the newspapers talked about 'settling scores', a phrase used when the people killed have already been condemned, even if the actual killing comes about through a quarrel over a woman or a car accident. It was assumed to begin with that the Scaglione affair was a one–off, but events proved otherwise. One after the other, a whole string of high-ranking officers, judges and politicians were blown away.[4] People read about it in the papers and couldn't believe it, yet one or two months later there would be another killing.

One headline in *Sicilia* read: 'The State under Attack'. I read the other papers too, to find out what they were thinking in Rome and up in the north, and they were all saying much the same thing. I couldn't believe they were that stupid. Where does attacking the state get anyone?

The truth of the matter was that while cigarettes and deals of that kind were the order of the day and some policeman or a magistrate decided to be awkward, it never occurred to anyone to liquidate him. For the sake of a few million lira it simply wasn't worth the hassle. It was all a matter of patience. Those who went to prison came out eventually and those who didn't were resigned to a lower income for a time. After a while everything was back to normal.

But with almost unlimited wealth at stake and life imprisonment with hard labour always on the cards, who would think twice about shooting? Did these police officers and magistrates really expect that they only had to say, 'Hey, scum, hand over that ten billion', and the man would hand over the ten billion and humbly beg forgiveness? If instead of staying tucked up in their warm offices those magistrates had taken a turn round the Quartiere della Kalsa or Tommaso Natale to see for themselves what real poverty and hunger were like, perhaps they would have been in a better position to understand certain things. When one of those lads had money in his pocket for the first time in his life, it was no good waving law books at him expecting him to come meekly to heel.

Everyone in Palermo was bribed, because money appeals to everyone. I saw Cosentino hand over rolls of banknotes to policemen, council officers and traffic wardens. And Stefano was friendly with senators, magistrates and mayors. And before Stefano, his father had had friends in Rome itself. Everyone got something, not only money, but favours, apartments, loans arranged with the banks, draft exemption for his sons, whatever he needed.

But there were certain judges and certain police officers who arrived with mainland airs and graces, paraded their haloes throughout Palermo and, on the strength of the occasional conviction, claimed arms, power and money. Dozens of innocent people were arrested on the pretext of 'First we'll send you to prison, then we'll argue about it'. Dozens of unfortunates who had done nothing at all were trampled underfoot, my poor wife among them. 'Honest' people can get away with this sort of thing with a clear conscience because no one can accuse them of taking backhanders. They don't do it for money, but in the name of Justice.

When people like the Kennedy brothers, the President of Egypt and Pope John Paul were being gunned down the world over, they were all convinced that no one would ever lift a finger against them, no matter what they did, and they probably died thinking: 'This can't be happening to me!'

Some of them were decent men and it was a shame they were killed. Two of these exceptional victims were known to me personally. One I only got to know shortly before his death, the other I had known for many years since he worked for the Doctor at Corleone. Purely out of respect for their families I won't mention their names. One certainly used his position to get the jobs he wanted for his sons, to dodge fines for himself and his friends, to have the use all day and every day of an official car and to stock his cellar with Christmas and New Year offerings. But he was basically an honest individual and never accepted a bribe from anyone. The other was a nonentity. Listening to him, even I, with my elementary education, understood that he was a nonentity. And lots of people in Palermo knew his wife, and not only by sight either. And the lady had another vice besides: poker, which she played at a well-known club, one frequented by the upper crust. Whenever there was an anonymous tip-off, the husband warned the wife and the wife warned her friends and when the police arrived everyone was chatting and playing bridge, which isn't a gambling game.

Now they are heroes, both having died on active service, and a plaque marks the spot where they were killed. When I went to read the words on the plaque it occurred to me that if there is such a thing as luck after death, these are two lucky men. In life they were nobodies, in death they are beyond the reach of criticism.

At the end of May 1978 Giuseppe Di Cristina was gunned down. It happened early in the morning, in Via Leonardo da Vinci. I was in hospital, not our own, but the official one. I had had an appendectomy and was still woozy when Cosentino came and told me what had happened, so I wasn't sure I had heard right.

'But why?' I asked when he'd finished. He pursed his lips.

'Who knows? It happened on Inzerillo's patch so poor Totuccio has got problems.'

Later I read that Di Cristina was a police spy, that he had provided them with the names of all the better known members of the Corleone group. I don't believe this. A more likely motive by far was the old friendship between him and the Bontate family. In one stroke they had removed a staunch ally of Stefano's and compromised another by carrying out the assassination on his territory.

'Is there nothing to go on?' I asked at length.

'Nothing so far. But all the signs point in one direction.'

'What has Stefano said?'

'The poor lad's very cut up. He's been discussing it with a lot of people. There are meetings all the time. I can't say any more yet: he's never at home. Even his wife was complaining.'

I had hoped to be out of hospital in a day or two, but when fate is against you there's nothing you can do about it. There were complications and I had to stay in for another fortnight. I therefore missed the son's funeral as well as the father's.

But I had time to think as I lay there in hospital. I thought about all those close to me who had died over the years, one after the other. I thought about each one separately, the good and the bad, the important ones and those who counted for nothing. In the end, the victors were always the men without principle, without faith, without honour, without dignity. The Corleonesi used to be just a small group of men; now they were finding allies and people to serve them everywhere. And those who were not prepared to ally themselves or to serve in their ranks met the same fate as Di Cristina.

This is the reason why I have never wanted to run my own outfit or give the orders to those I worked with. There have been times when I was asked to do this, but I have always refused. Time was when I would have accepted, but then I learnt better and it was Di Cristina himself who helped me to learn. He had once said jokingly that there was no longer a place for university–educated men. I say that there was no longer a place for anyone except the Corleonesi. The future was to prove me right and the fact that I am still alive today is largely due to my having realized this before many others did.

Notes

1. Afflicted in heart and pocket.
2. A speciality of Palermo.
3. *Salma*: a Sicilian land measurement.
4. These included Colonel Russo, Senator Reina, Judge Terranova, Captain Basile and Senator Mattarella.

XVI

In the summer of '79 something very odd happened. Not being the curious type, I thought nothing of it at the time and a week later had forgotten all about it. It was only much later that I was reminded of the incident.

It was a Sunday. I remember that because the day was a scorcher and I had gone to the beach with a couple of friends: Gambino, who died of cancer a few years ago, and a guy called Saro who was nicknamed *Menzapinna*,[1] because of an operation he had had as a kid. Sara and I were *la stessa cosa*[2] also where the sea was concerned. Like me, he couldn't swim and no one could teach him. So while the others splashed around and had fun in the sea, he and I waded along with the water up to our bellies, keeping a wary eye on the waves. And we had a pact, that if one of us slipped or was pushed over, the other would come to his rescue.

I got a message that Stefano himself wanted to see me. I rang him at once and he told me to get over to his house straight away. At that time he was staying in the country with his family at Magliocco, a small village. When I arrived he was sitting under a tree, wearing a singlet. He pulled up a folding stool for me, like the camp stools people use on the beach.

'Now, Giovannino, listen carefully. There's going to be a meeting this week in Spartola's office. I don't know the exact day yet. Be prepared to get there in fifteen minutes flat . . . '

I assumed it was to be a bodyguard job, but I was

175

wrong. I had to find out if the meeting was under surveillance, and when it ended I had to follow the guest of honour and see if his car was being tailed. Easy. The worst part was having to sit at home by the phone in that heat which didn't even ease off at night. I had acquired a taste for beer and was opening one can after another. At last the call came.

The man in question was small and thin, with hollow cheeks and only a few white hairs on an otherwise bald head. He was followed in by Stefano and then Totò Inzerillo who was scowling – but then he always scowled. Then another man arrived, a man with a moustache who spoke loudly with a Catanese drawl. He was arm in arm with a man I knew vaguely by sight; I think he was a councillor in the Mattarella administration, Mattarella still being alive then. I didn't see any others go in, though there were more when they came out so some must have got there before I did.

Stefano's suspicions were justified because I soon saw a face I recognized in a bar close by. I couldn't think of the man's name to begin with, but when I reported later it came back to me: Marchese. As soon as the meeting started he went to find a telephone, making a call which lasted half a minute or less. He had a motor bike, which was by now the only means of following a car in Palermo without losing it in the traffic, and at the end of the meeting latched on to the tail of the car carrying the man with the hollow cheeks. When the car pulled into the drive of an attractive villa just outside the city, the motor cyclist noted the house number and the name of the road and left. I waited for ten minutes and then left too.

But that wasn't the end of the matter. Stefano met the man again, this time on his own. As his driver was off sick it was up to me to drive Stefano; no one had said anything to the contrary, so I assumed they were going back to the same villa, but when Stefano realized this, he tapped me on the shoulder.

'Where are you going, Giovannino? Turn round, go back to Via Notarbartolo.'

The other man kept running his tongue over his lips. He spoke in a thin, high–pitched voice that sounded like a goat bleating, and he stammered every now and then.

'There's no need to worry,' said Stefano eventually, 'we'll take care of this ourselves. No problem. Ah, if only all problems were as easy . . . ' Then he said something about the Punta Raisi Airport and mentioned a certain Coniglio, or Conigliaro, who worked there. At last he asked the man what he had decided to do.

'I'm waiting for a reply. Can I ring you tomorrow afternoon?'

'I'll ring you; it's better that way,' replied Stefano, and told me to pull in outside an old palazzo. A blue Alfetta was waiting there with a man at the wheel and two more sitting in the back. The man at the wheel leapt out quickly and came to open the door of our car. Greetings and goodbyes took some time and when the others had all left Stefano breathed a sigh of relief.

'With any luck we'll have no more hassle from that quarter. Let's go to see Calogero Pizzuto, Giovannino. Do you know where he lives?'

'*Voscenza no.*'

'I'll direct you. Drive.'

As I said before, it was only very much later that I happened to glance at a copy of *Ora*. There was a photograph of Michele Sindona[3] who was serving a long sentence in an American gaol. An Italian judge had ordered his extradition to Italy. One glance was enough: this was the man I had driven to Via Notarbartolo.

*

It was a year full of strange happenings. Fate seemed to be having fun at my expense, testing me to see whether I was capable of working in the dark, neither seeing or hearing a thing.

The next time my orders came from Cosentino. He drove me in his own car to a spot just outside Palermo, in a district that I knew next to nothing about. He pointed out a modern, white–painted villa and told me there was a small wood–framed window at the rear that could easily be opened. As soon as it began to get dark I was to enter the house and station myself behind the front door. Perhaps (and his voice rose on the 'perhaps' and he spread out his hands), perhaps someone would arrive. They might arrive at ten o'clock, at eleven o'clock, or midnight, but whatever happened I was to stay there until daybreak.

'And if this person does arrive, what then?' I asked. Cosentino made the usual sign with his right hand.

'One shot only. But make it a good one.'

I didn't ask what I was supposed to do if five people turned up instead of one, or if the one who turned up happened to be a child or a bishop or a friend of the Family. The only doubt Cosentino had expressed was about the person coming to the villa or not. There was nothing else I needed to know. Cosentino had a slightly rough and ready way with him but he was more meticulous than a German, and when Mimmo Teresi wanted to tease him he actually called him '*u tedescu* or sometimes *Musulinu*.[4] But Teresi could get away with it. He was a high–ranking member of the Family and also related to Stefano.

'When is it to be?'

'Maybe tomorrow. Stay at home by the phone every afternoon. I'll give you a call.'

Nothing happened for four days. When it did, I was

good and rested after four afternoons spent doing little but sleep. But all the same I prepared a flask of strong coffee and then left straight away. I wanted to find a good place to leave the 127. If the man turned up I didn't want him put on his guard by the sight of a car parked in front of the villa.

It was nearly dark when I got into the house but as the shutters were raised I could see well enough and I had a good look round. This wasn't idle curiosity: I was trying to get acquainted with the basic geography of the place. It had class – you could see that at a glance. And although the fridge was turned off, the owners obviously used the house quite often because all the beds were made and it was spotless.

Every now and then a car passed, every now and then I heard voices, and each time I stationed myself behind the front door. It was December and very cold, so the coffee came in handy more for keeping warm than for keeping awake. Although I usually go to bed early, I can always stay awake easily if I have to. It was around one o'clock when I heard a car pull up outside. The light from the headlamps showed under the door. But there was no sound of a car door being slammed. It stayed there for well over a minute with the engine running, then left.

At five I got ready to leave. I went to a first–floor window and had a good look round to see if there was any movement or maybe a car parked somewhere near. There was nothing. I waited another twenty minutes just to be on the safe side, then left the same way I came, and when I got back to the 127 I found the door had been forced and the radio stolen.

I read things about that villa later in the Palermo press, but to this day I still don't know why I was sent there or who I was waiting for.

But another villa was waiting for me, though the

circumstances would be rather different this time. At Stefano's invitation, Don Masino Buscetta[5] and his family were staying in a villa belonging to the Salvo family on the road between Palermo and Messina, quite close to the Zagarella, a hotel where I had often delivered goods and collected money. There were three villas there. Saro *Menzapinna* and I were to keep a discreet eye on the middle one throughout the Christmas holiday period. There was no danger because Don Masino's presence was being kept a very close secret, but one can never be too careful. A guard was already there but he left as soon as we arrived. The Federico brothers were around right at the beginning, and on the first evening Cosentino paid a brief visit, but after that there were only the two of us, chosen because neither of us had a family so it was all the same to us if we spent the festive season surrounded by lemon trees and sleeping in the garage.

I saw Stefano a couple of times, too, but he was always in company; the first time he had a woman with him who, from a distance, looked like his wife. Nino Salvo also turned up, in a Range Rover, a vehicle I didn't know he owned. When he saw me standing near the gate he got out and came over for a chat.

'What are they talking about in there?' he asked first, pointing towards the villa with his nose. I explained that I was only there as a guard and never went into the house itself.

'Just as well the weather's not cold, then.'

'You Palermo guys don't know what cold is,' I said, and he laughed. We exchanged a few quips, then he got back into the car.

'In case I don't see you again, happy New Year.'

'And the same to you, *Voscenza*. With all that's happening at the moment, we need a good year.'

'Don't I know it!' he replied. And he wasn't laughing any more.

Cosentino arrived on the 31st and informed us that a hot meal was going to be brought over from the hotel.

'Let's hope there's some for us too,' said Saro. Cosentino frowned at him. I was fond of Saro, but he had his limitations. He didn't understand that one should never ask for things because if one was going to get them one got them, and if one was not going to get them asking wouldn't do any good. But certain subtleties were beyond him and it was useless trying to explain them. Apart from this he was good company, full of affection and respect. When it was windy or cold he always offered to go out and do a tour of inspection even if it was my turn.

Once when I was out doing a tour, I caught sight of Don Masino, the only time in my life I ever saw him. He had his wife with him, a slender platinum blonde. She looked very elegant and much younger than him; I had heard she came from a rich and powerful family. I also knew that Don Masino had quite a reputation as a lady–killer. That day they were chatting away and seemed very jolly. No one so much as dreamt of what would happen later, the trial and the revelations he would make. The courts and the journalists talked of him as a *pentito*,[6] the Corleonesi called him a lot of quite different things. I heard him speak on the television and read some of his statements in the press.

What can I say about him? Don Masino had found himself alone. Like me. And in an American gaol. By breaking silence he avenged his dead friends, and he has explained why he could no longer consider those he accused as men of honour. By doing what he did he may have ensured his own liberty, at least in the short term. I believe that there was a point when he realized that without either the arms or the men to make the

Corleonesi pay for their crimes, the only way he could bring them to their knees was by spilling the beans in court. And that is precisely what he did.

Certain things in his statements made me realize that he was undoubtedly in the confidence of some of the most important men in the Palermo Families. For example, I had known nothing about the quarrels between Stefano and his brother Giovanni. I never met Giovanni. I knew he was the younger of the two and that he and Stefano never got on because Giovanni was jealous. All I remember is that when he was arrested in the spring of 1980, Cosentino remarked that Stefano was well rid of a pain in the backside. Panno, an oldish man I saw now and then, was with him at the time and laughed when he heard this, so I knew he agreed with it. None of this made any sense to me so I kept my mouth shut.

But while I listened I remembered an incident that had taken place some time earlier. There had been an election in the Family. Saro told me about it. I didn't believe him, I thought it was just one of those daft things Saro used to say to pass the time. What did he mean by elections? Stefano wasn't a deputy who could be voted out of office and replaced by someone else! Saro told me he had heard about it from Ignazio Pullarà, who had discussed it with him because he wanted to persuade him to vote against Stefano. The rival party was strong and had support both inside and outside the Family. But Saro was frightened; he had said he wanted to think about it and they had never approached him again.

I thought about all these things during the night while I guarded the villa where the Buscetta family slept. And on New Year's Eve, after a good meal and a half bottle of sweet spumante the guard had brought us with the compliments of Nino Salvo, I asked Saro to tell me how the election business had ended.

'Ah, yes. Cosentino wanted you to vote too. Didn't he tell you?'

I knew nothing about it. Saro explained that Cosentino, certain of my loyalty, had known that my vote was secure. But the others had reminded him of the rules. Who was I? They hardly knew me. Some of them had never even heard my name. So in the end the matter was dropped. Stefano, after all, had won just the same.

'And what did he do then?' I asked. I felt really put out. In his place I should have made short work of those bastards. How can one feel safe knowing that there are people around who've got it in for you? Even if you're democratically elected.

'How should I know? Nothing. Nothing happened. Everyone was as friendly as before.'

We drank toast after toast until two in the morning, but I was anything but merry. I had a hunch that 1981, which everyone was now welcoming with popping corks and thunderflashes, was going to be a disaster for me and for others.

And so it proved.

Notes

1. *Menzapinna* – 'Half–penis': probably circumcised.

2. *La stessa cosa*: literally 'the same thing', a traditional Mafia expression denoting members of the same Family.

3. *Michele Sindona*: this Sicilian financier had close links with various local and American Mafia groups, and was related politically to Giulio Andreotti, the Christian Democrat politician. After the collapse of his Franklin National Bank he was arrested in the USA. In Italy he was charged with the premeditated murder of the liquidator of the Banca Privata Italiana, which was also owned by him and also collapsed

in 1974. (See *Mafia Business* by Pino Arlacchi, translated by Martin Ryle, OUP, 1988.)

4. 'The German' or 'Mussolini'.

5. Tommaso Buscetta: a *mafioso* from Palermo active in Sicily, Canada and in Latin America from 1960 onwards. After the extermination of the greater part of his immediate family and his *cosca* by the rival Greco–Corleonesi *cosche* between 1981 and 1984, Buscetta decided to collaborate with the investigators, breaking the long tradition of official silence and covert collaboration maintained by all the Sicilian bosses. (See Pino Arlacchi, *Op. cit.*, p.66.)

6. *Pentito*: one who has changed his mind, a reformed character.

XVII

Yet the year began well enough. There was a huge unexpected windfall of 'dirty' money, which some people jokingly referred to as *munnizza*, garbage. But this was golden garbage because you could buy it for a half, a third, or even – when the risk was very high – for a quarter of its value. There weren't too many takers, either, at the time: some preferred to steer clear of this kind of deal, some had problems of their own, some were short of the readies. So, as it turned out, it was left to me and only a few others to share the cake between us.

I stashed the money in a safe box at a bank in Agrigento owned by some friends. My contact there, thanks to Cosentino, was the late lamented Calogero Pizzuto from San Giovanni Gemini. He accompanied me personally to the manager of the bank and saw that everything was done properly. When I stopped over at the village on the way back to Palermo, I felt like the emperor of China. In three days, had I wanted to, I could have bought a hundred hectares of good land and a big house in the high street. But it never occurred to me to do anything as daft. Hardly anyone there even knew me now, and I wanted the few who saw me around from time to time to accept me as one of the many emigrants who keep up an occasional contact with the village in the hope that one day they will be able to retire to the place where they were born.

Quite a surprising thing happened while I was there. Much against my will, my cousin persuaded me to accept an invitation to Sunday dinner. There were about fifteen people present and I was uncomfortable because I hate large gatherings, and anyway I was only used to speaking, eating and chatting with people of my own set. But as I couldn't very well refuse, I turned up at the appointed hour. Next to me was a woman of about forty, dressed in black, a friend of my cousin's wife. Her name was Crocefissa, the same as my mother's, but everyone called her Fina or Finuzza. She had a small child with her who sat at the table just like a grown-up and was no trouble at all.

When the meal was over, my cousin – who had downed a whole flask of wine as usual – took my arm, more for support than out of affection, and steered me on to the little veranda. It was a clear day and you could see right across the countryside to the mountains in the distance.

'Now, what do you think of Finuzza?' he asked at once. I immediately thought he must be screwing her and wanted to brag about it. She was a widow, and this is generally what happens to widows unless they remarry. But I was wrong. They were after me as a prospective husband for Finuzza!

I wanted to laugh, but refrained: my cousin's wife was a good sort and I didn't want to offend her. Both she and my cousin wanted to fix me up with a wife willy-nilly. They kept saying I should take the plunge before I was fifty because after that it would be too late and I should have to take what I could get. What could be better than a widow from a decent family without a whole lot of children? My cousin's wife praised Finuzza's personality and her husband swore (with his hand on his heart) that there had never been a breath of scandal about her in the village.

'And she's a fine-looking woman. Did you notice?'
'I did.'

'And she's only forty, in fact she's not yet had her fortieth birthday.'

I didn't try to find out if my cousins were trying to do a favour to their friends, or to me, or if there was any other ulterior motive. I cut the discussion short by inventing a girlfriend in Palermo and saying that we were thinking of getting married in a year's time when certain things were sorted out on my side. I thanked them for their concern, but said that it would have been dishonourable for me to raise false hopes in the breast of a nice lady like Finuzza. And that was that.

On my return to Palermo I found Cosentino ill. The doctors were baffled: his temperature kept going up and down for no apparent reason and he had to lie down the whole time. I went round straight away. There were some people with him, but as soon as I arrived they excused themselves and disappeared into another room. His wife brought me a coffee and then left us alone, he resting with his head raised on a couple of pillows, I sitting at the foot of the bed.

'I was expecting you, Giovannino . . . '

There was a score to be settled. A few days previously the Corleonesi had gunned down Piddu Panno at Casteldaccia. Did I remember Panno, an oldish man? He had a small villa in the country, near Stefano's place.

'*Voscenza sì.*'

Stefano had been fond of the old man, who had been a friend of his father's. And he had decided that the time had come to tell that lot to call a halt and go back to the rule books. He wanted Totò Riina taken care of once and for all and there was only one way of catching him off his guard: at a meeting of bosses.

I came out in a cold sweat. Salvatore Riina was officially a fugitive from justice. They were doing their best, poor bastards, no one could deny that; but no matter how hard they looked, they could never find him. They probably thought here was Totò, an old man of over fifty; he must be sick and tired of hiding out in rough huts with only rats for company; sooner or later he would up and turn himself in.

In fact he was moving around Palermo as freely as I was. Every now and then I ran into someone who had seen him. But no one knew where the hideout was, and I personally believe that he was changing it all the time. That was going to make it exceedingly difficult to set a trap, and that was why Stefano had thought up the scheme of taking him totally by surprise and picking him off when they were all sitting down together.

But it was sheer madness. Certain death! There was no way the gunman could get away alive. I said as much to Cosentino. He took some time before replying.

'You may be right or you may not; there is certainly a great deal of risk involved. And for that reason D'Agostino has come up with a plan. Each *suttacapu*,[1] acting independently and in secret, will organize a small team or act alone or possibly engage someone. It's up to him. And he will say nothing to anyone else. That way the thing will be kept secret.'

The word secrecy reminded me immediately of what Saro *Menzapinna* had told me about his conversations with Pullarà before the elections. I had to tell Cosentino about it. If Pullarà was to be one of those entrusted with secrecy, the cat would be out of the bag in no time.

'Bullshit, absolute bullshit,' replied Cosentino. Yes, there had been rivalries within the Family, but more apparent than real. Saro was an idiot to listen to that sort of thing. There had never been traitors amongst us. Discussions of course, all the time, but discussion and betrayal are two very different things.

'Do you know how often Stefano and I have disagreed? Times without number. But does this mean I would sell him out to the Corleonesi?'

'*Voscenza no.*'

'Good man. Now listen . . . '

I began to sweat again. Cosentino, as cell leader, had decided to entrust this job to me. Not alone: I had to find one or at the most two men to help, the choice was mine. He didn't even need to know them. And since I was rather gentlemanly in my use of fire-arms, one at least of my companions should be capable of handling a machine–gun, which is sometimes the only choice available. I was to tell him when I was ready and then he would let me know where to go.

All this talk of secrecy could, I realized, mean only one thing. Cosentino knew that there were traitors in the Family. He had denied it in order to set my mind at rest. But I knew him too well after all these years and could tell he was worried. And a thought struck me. If he distrusted Pullarà and certain others, how come the plan had been discussed so openly at a meeting of the cell bosses? Riina would have heard about it in fifteen minutes flat. So, I reasoned, this was Cosentino's own baby. He had given me, and perhaps others besides, the order to go after Riina to forestall an attempt by Stefano himself. And he was right: what is a soldier's life worth compared to that of the general?

I left, and spent a lot of time pacing up and down with my hands in my pockets. Apart from Saro, there was only one person I could trust and who was a stranger to Palermo. Mariano wasn't his real name, but that's what I'll call him. He came from Riesi and was the son of a man who had worked for Giuseppe Di Cristina. I had got to know him in Riesi and later he came to visit me at home. He was anxious to get on in the world and although he was still very young, you could tell from the way he spoke that he was intelligent and had a good head on his shoulders. Besides, people who come from the country districts still have a sense of honour and respect. It's cities that turn men into brutes.

I looked him up and asked him a few questions – without revealing anything of the matter in hand, naturally. I was only testing the water. If he were not willing, I had already decided to ask Carmelo, the fellow who had handled the Lucia business. But Mariano was happy to work with me.

Then I went to tell Saro. Cosentino would have disapproved the move, but I knew my man. Saro loved me like a dog loves his master. He had never had any family: a bastard himself, he had never wanted to marry because he was afraid of being cuckolded. He had told me this in confidence one evening, making me swear that I would never tell another soul. I was his family.

'*Comu veni si cunta*,'² Saro said when I told him about the business.

'Are you game?'

'I think it's sheer suicide. But today or tomorrow, you have to die sometime.'

I cheered him up by taking him to a good restaurant in the centre of town where he had never been before, and ordered things he had never tasted in his life. When he drank he slurped noisily and some of the other diners turned round and gave him black looks. He noticed this and tried to be more careful, but I told him not to mind.

'Don't worry, *Sariddu*, if they dare say a word, they'll find themselves paying our bill as well as their own.'

At the beginning of April I was approached by a certain Lanza. I already knew him by sight and knew that in his time he had been a *uomo di rispetto* in Croceverde Giardini. But he was no longer anyone to be reckoned with, even though he gave himself airs. He was too old. His nickname was *Ciancianedda*, 'Tinkerbell', but I've no idea why.

While I was not particularly worried to find him suddenly on my doorstep, I couldn't think of any reason for it. And when he explained I didn't believe him. The Commission had decided to close its file on Stefano Bontate, and I was actually expected to act as executioner. Confronted with certain situations that defy credibility, you sometimes think people are having you on. But in a matter as serious as this, not even Don Calò Vizzini in his prime would have tried to joke, let alone an old goat like Lanza.

Even after all those years I still didn't understand how some things worked. The little I know about Commissions, *Cupole*,[3] and that sort of thing was gleaned from reading the papers, and God alone knows how much of it is true. For myself, on the few occasions when I have heard people I know gossiping about such things, I have changed the subject at once if possible, and if it wasn't possible I have closed my ears and mouth and thought my own thoughts. So while other people were looking at the sky to see how God and his angels were passing the time, I kept my eyes on the ground to avoid stepping into the shit.

That evening a few of us had arranged to meet for supper. But who could think about food at a time like this? I went down to the beach to look at the sea and think. I was a dead man. If I refused to obey my days were counted. If I told Stefano the result would be the same. What could he do to help, he who never knew when he got up in the morning if he still had a whole day ahead of him or not? If I agreed to do the job, they would come at me from both sides. Not that it even entered my head to agree. Whatever happened, I intended to die with my hands clean.

What I failed to understand was the reason. I had heard once or twice that there were traitors in the Family, maybe several, and that this was the reason for the upsets, since someone among these traitors was close to Stefano and even related to him. My conversation with Cosentino had confirmed these rumours. But why had they chosen someone like me for the job? I thought about it all night long and got nowhere. The following day I ran into Mimmo Teresi and one of the others I had been supposed to have supper with.

'You're looking green around the gills, Giovannino. Are you ill?'

'Stomach upset. I've been up all night.'

'Was that why you didn't turn up yesterday evening?' asked the other.

'Yes.'

'You might have let us know. We were worried.'

He was right. With things as they were, anyone who failed to turn up on time made the friends who were waiting for him fear the worst. Then Teresi, who had a great regard for me, said something which, although he didn't realize it, opened my eyes.

'You must get better quickly. Men who can be trusted may be needed at any moment.'

That's what I was: a man to be trusted. And I'm proud of it. It's what I've always wanted and what I've always been: *un uomo d'onore*, loyal through and through. And therefore one whom Stefano would never suspect. Even now, I still reckon that this was the reason why Lanza was sent to me. Had I agreed, I would have had access to Stefano; had I refused, they would have had proof positive of my feelings towards the Family and would have known that they had to get rid of me.

I had a few days' grace in which to put my affairs in order and decide whether to ask Cosentino's advice or resolve the problem on my own as I always did. Luckily Stefano was extremely busy at the time and hardly anyone saw him alone. People were saying he was tired and had lost heart.

I listened to such gossip with only one ear. My mind was constantly busy and my eyes open to all that was going on. I had decided to wait and see. Something new was happening every other moment and sooner or later the wind would change. Our orders were to be ready day and night, so something big was definitely afoot.

'At last, by the grace of God, we're going to get some action,' said Mimmo Teresi. The time for talking was over, in other words, and no one could have been happier about it than I was, because while the others were all suffering from a sense of approaching danger, my doom was sealed. My skin would only be saved if war broke out and we won it. And meanwhile I held Saro and Mariano in readiness. As soon as Cosentino had definite news about Riina, we were to go into action.

But that wasn't how things worked out.

On the evening of 23 April we were all at Stefano's house in the country celebrating his forty–third birthday. When he drove off I left the party immediately because I had some personal business to see to. It was nearly midnight when this was finished, but I wasn't at all tired. In fact I was feeling so lively that I decided to pay a surprise visit to someone I saw from time to time. This was Teresa, a nice lady with one small child. Her husband worked in Switzerland as a waiter and only came home in the summer and for a few days at Christmas and Easter. He didn't want her with him in Switzerland, he said, because official permits were hard to come by. I suspect the real reason was another nice lady with another small child in Switzerland, and the waiter preferred to keep his two families apart.

I always went at night, because in the daytime neighbours would have seen me and the child would have been around. No need to ring doorbells and wake the neighbourhood: I opened the door with my own key and went in. In the morning I left around six. A peasant and the child of peasants, getting up early has never been a problem, winter or summer. When I left Teresa I always drove home slowly; if it was summer I would stop for a *granita* along the way, or a brioche *alla palermitana*, filled with ice–cream; in the winter I would have a cappuccino. That particular day I caught a whiff of freshly baked bread and bought a small loaf still hot from the oven to eat in comfort as soon as I got home.

The phone was ringing as I opened the door. It was one of the Federico brothers, I don't remember which, but his voice was so distorted by panic that I didn't recognize it at first.

'*L'ammazzaru! L'ammazzaru!* – They've killed him! They've killed him!' he shouted over and over again. I told him to calm down because I couldn't understand what he was saying, but he wasn't even listening. Eventually he managed to speak: Stefano was dead. They had shot him the evening before while he was on his way back from the party. The car was standing at a traffic light. I knew he had ordered a car with bullet–proof glass, an Alfa Romeo I believe, and it was to be delivered within a day or two. But maybe not even bullet–proof glass could have protected him from a Kalashnikov.

I leapt to my feet. There was no time to think. I took nothing but money, the pistol and the keys of the 127. The bread stayed on the kitchen table, cooling.

I did some shopping in a supermarket in Viale

Strasburgo. The only other customers were housewives and a few old-age pensioners. I chose all kinds of tinned food, long-life milk, dried sweetmeats, nuts, wine. As for fresh food, I only bought stuff which would last for some time in the fridge. Then I bought an electric razor, a radio and a few bits and pieces. By the time I had finished, the boot of the car was stuffed to capacity. It was now ten o'clock; I had the rest of the day in front of me and I had to find a safe place to spend it. There are only two safe places: the middle of a crowd or somewhere absolutely deserted. But the sea was always the place I thought of first and I had noticed that no one ever pays much attention to a man fishing or just staring at the sea. Parking the car beside a wooden hut so that it was almost completely invisible from the road, I spent the whole day sitting on a rock watching the old men with their rods and buckets.

When it grew dark they all left, but I stayed for a while, thinking of nothing at all. I was going to have plenty of time for thinking. I shut my eyes and breathed in the sea air, which to me is the air of freedom. That, for some time to come, was going to be in short supply.

A wind got up at around one in the morning. I noticed the trees starting to bend before it as I drove through the Parco della Favorita. When I reached Mondello paper bags and empty cigarette packets were blowing about all over the place and there was not a soul to be seen. I had had my eye on one little beach house for four years, and now its time had come. It belonged to a civil engineer from Turin who arrived every year at the beginning of August and stayed the whole month. I had checked repeatedly: he never came at Christmas, never in the spring, only in August.

The other beach houses were all in darkness. I had the door open in a twinkling, carried everything inside and returned to the car. At two o'clock I abandoned the 127 in front of the station and helped myself to an Alfetta. As I drove back through the park it occurred to me that any road–block would be the end of me. I'm not a fast driver and certainly could not have shaken them off if they chased me. My one hope would be to pelt on foot for the cover of the trees. But at that late hour and with that high wind everyone was in bed. I left the Alfetta quite a long distance from the beach house and walked the rest of the way. It was now dawn, on 25 April, and I remained in that beach house, without once turning on a light or opening a window, until 17 July, while in the world outside the members of the Family were being wiped out one by one.

I still find myself thinking from time to time of those eighty–four days of voluntary imprisonment which saved my life and brought me very near to madness.

By day I thought, by night I dreamt, and eventually the two became confused. To begin with I thought only of him, *'u carusu*[4] as the older members of the Family used to call him, those who had seen him as a boy in short trousers in the days when his father was one of the most important men in Palermo. They knew, too, what he had done for his sick, bed–ridden father, for his uncle who was afflicted with the same illness, for his brother, for his friends, for everyone who needed something from him. Stefano had been a real man, generous and good, too good for those Judases.

Then I was tempted to take my pistol and go out late at night to pick off a few of them. I knew a lot of the small fry, I knew where they hung out and how their minds worked. It would have been easy. But as far as the others were concerned, not even the Almighty could have found them. Sometimes I would hear cars draw up outside the beach house at night. The weather was already hot, the bathers were about. Every time I heard a car door slam I ran to look through a slit in the shutters.

Meanwhile, my imagination was working overtime. Were they looking for me? The radio kept me informed about who was already dead and who had got away like me. Inzerillo's death made me realize that the massacre would continue until not a single one of us was at large. Not even the bullet–proof car had saved him. It must have been the one ordered by Stefano. But no one can spend all his time in a bullet–proof car, and he had been gunned down as he walked through a door.

I didn't miss a news bulletin, and all the news was bad. *Cascittuni* was killed, shot in his own bed. *'Nzino* too, shot together with Carmelo. It was wholesale slaughter. There was no hope. The war was over before it started. We hadn't even entered it and we had already lost it because everyone else had sided with the Corleonesi. And the only news on the radio was about deaths. They knew nothing about those like me who had scattered, and I didn't know if they had gone looking for me at Teresa's, in the village or at my flat, or if they had found the 127 and assumed I had got away by train.

I thought about my two rooms and my belongings. Had they all been chucked about? There was a photograph of my father wearing a bow tie which I had put in a silver frame and kept on the table beside my bed. I imagined it torn, or lying on the floor face down. Maybe it was sitting on the desk of some commissioner of police, or in the hands of God knows who . . .

Tinned food started to drive me crazy. I couldn't bear to eat the stuff without bread any longer. After a certain age, fresh bread is more important than a woman. The day I had spent hiding in the drum, in that terrible heat and with fear gnawing at my vitals, had been better than the two and a half months I spent in the beach house at Mondello. I had reached the point of talking to myself and laughing aloud, and I had let my beard grow, although I cannot stand hair on my face. So one night at the end of June I decided to slip out for a moment.

My knees were shaking. I took short steps like an old man and whenever I passed anyone I scratched my nose or my forehead so they couldn't see my face properly. It was now high summer; there were still people about even at that late hour and they were all sporting fine suntans. I went close enough to the sea to smell it. There were no waves, not a breath of wind. Then I saw an all–night fruit stall; it was selling slices of iced water–melon, and after the first slice I could have eaten another ten; but the stall–holder was already giving me curious looks because I was gulping the stuff down like an animal, and I didn't want to give him a reason for remembering me. I bought everything I could carry and returned to the beach house feeling childishly happy. But I never went out again.

The fresh air had done me good, however. I started to think again and see things more clearly. The most important thing, the one that mattered most, was that nobody would come after Stefano. I didn't want to work for anyone else. All I wanted was to stay alive, and if I succeeded my life would have to change. Now I realize that it was the solitude and the tension making me think like that. It wasn't up to me whether I lived or died. Not even those who had gone into hiding abroad could be sure of getting away with it, much less myself whose only friends were in Palermo and maybe they were all dead by now. Even so, I continued to gaze out on the street every evening when it was dark, always with the one thought in my mind, that my life would have to change.

On 16 July I spent the whole day putting everything straight. A woman would have noticed that someone had been there, but the engineer was a widower and lived alone. A male, an engineer and a Torinese, what could he be expected to notice, poor devil! Late at night I got rid of all the rubbish before going to bed, the next morning I shaved off my beard and walked out on to the street like anyone else, had a coffee and caught the bus into town. It was one of the best journeys of my life.

No one was expecting me to appear out of the blue. Those who had searched for me would think I was far away, while the others would be assuming I was dead. For a little while I had the advantage. I got to the Eden bar at around ten o'clock. There were a few customers there already but no one of any importance. *Testa munnata* was busy washing a glass and glanced at me as if there was nothing out of the ordinary.

'Ah, Giovannino, back again?'

'Back again. What's the latest?'

'Nothing new . . . Ah, someone's been asking for you.'

He had said: *ti cercano*. I looked at him to make sure I had understood. *Ti cercano* means one thing; *ti stanno cercando* means something quite different.[5]

'Who's been asking for me?' I enquired. He was leaning on the counter. Now he came closer and whispered a name and a nickname. I had never met the man but I knew who he was and who he worked for. He had been asking for news of me, wanting to know what had happened to me. Someone less familiar with the scene might have assumed this was a trick to force me into the open, but I knew differently. Leaving messages with barmen is not the way to achieve certain results. I put the money for my drink on the counter.

'*Salutamu.*'

'*Ni viremu.*'[6]

I had nothing to do until the evening, and as I couldn't go to the flat, I went for a good walk and then, around noon, decided to pay Teresa a visit. After all, the child wasn't going to catch measles if he saw me for once. To be on the safe side I decided not to use my key, but as I rang the bell I noticed a new name beside it. The door was opened by a tiny woman with watery eyes.

'Is the *signora* in?' I asked.

She knew nothing about her, had never even met her. She lived with her old widowed mother. The flat had been empty when they moved in. It had been a stroke of luck for two women on their own with little money. The only way of finding out whether they were speaking the truth was to put the fear of God into them, although I knew already that they were too simple—minded to be acting a part. I made them wet their pants but got nowhere: they had told me all they knew. They were blubbing as I left, and I hadn't laid a finger on them.

I could do nothing else all day. There was no porter in the block so I asked questions left right and centre; tenants, shopkeepers, neighbours, the lot. No one could tell me a thing, and this was hardly surprising because Teresa lived very quietly and wasn't even a local woman by birth.

Later, when things had got back nearer to normal, I investigated some more, even making inquiries at the Town Hall, but their records only showed her as living at the old address.

In the end I gave up. And I never saw Teresa again.

Notes

1. *Suttacapu*: cell leader.
2. What will be will be.
3. *Coppola*: Member of a Mafia organization (from the flat, peaked cap worn by Sicilian peasants).
4. *'u carusu*: the young one.
5. *'Ti stanno cercando'* implies someone is looking for you with a gun; *'ti cercano'* means they want to talk to you.
6. *'Salutamu . . . Ni viremu'* 'Cheers . . . See you around.'

XVIII

The person who had been looking for me was Nino Salvo. He and his cousin Ignazio controlled all the tax offices in Sicily; they were also connected with top men such as senators in Rome and Palermo, construction company bosses and captains of industry. A force to be reckoned with.

The bond between Stefano and the Salvo cousins went deeper than that of common interest. Especially between Nino and Stefano there had also been mutual respect and affection. And this was the first subject Nino touched on when we met:

'Things will never be the same again without Stefano. The world's falling apart, Giovannino.'

I had phoned him and been asked to meet him at his place. He had a beautiful house, full of valuable things. We sat on a sofa. He was curious to know where I had been hiding for so long with no help from anyone and no access to news.

'I had a battery radio – while the batteries lasted . . . '

'Did you hear about Totuccio Inzerillo?'

'*Voscenza sì.*'

But he wasn't the only one they'd done away with. Totuccio and Angelo Federico were dead, so was Giuseppe Di Francesco. Mimmo Teresi had disappeared and Emanuele D'Agostino soon afterwards. They'd tried to get Contorno, but he, at least, had managed to escape.

'And Cosentino?'

'They've clapped him in the Ucciardone. And he's in for keeps.'

'Does the Family as such still exist?' I asked. Salvo looked at me in a strange way, then nodded his head.

'Lo Jacono has been made regent. He and the Pullarà brothers are giving the orders now.'

Vernengo and Saccone, among others, were still around too, in fact all those who had voted against Stefano in those wretched elections. The others were all dead or had vanished or escaped, while they were carrying on calmly as if nothing had happened and no one had touched a hair of their heads. I looked at Salvo.

'They've pulled it off, huh?'

'Indeed. And if you want to know who betrayed Inzerillo, ask who's running his Family now. There's a Judas round every corner these days, enough and to spare.'

I asked about Saro *Menzapinna*. He had never even heard the name. He called for coffee and then began to speak. A friend of the Salvos' had just gone missing, obviously the work of the other lot. This was Lo Presti – a civil engineer and Nino's cousin, if I'm not mistaken. Lo Presti was a really big shot in Palermo, he'd had a finger in every pie. This fact alone, if you could read the signs, meant that all those who had sided with Bontate and Inzerillo were finished. The Salvo cousins, because of their financial pull, were possibly not in danger, but fear doesn't make for a clear head.

At last he put his cards on the table. He wanted a bodyguard, a man he could trust, someone who knew his way around. I fitted the bill on all counts and he wanted me to be his secretary cum armed guard. I liked the proposal but I wanted to know what I would be getting in return. And it wasn't a question of money.

'For a while you must keep clear, Giovannino. Take your time to get yourself organized. Meanwhile I'll put the word around that you're with me now. You'll see, out of respect or self–interest they'll leave you alone. They've got nothing personal against you, have they?'

I said no, hoping that my search for Totò Riina had remained a secret between me and Cosentino, because if that had got around not even a dozen Salvo cousins would have been enough to protect me.

'Come back in a fortnight . . . if we're still alive,' he said, and within five minutes I was walking through the crowds in Palermo with my hands in my pockets and my head buzzing. And I was alive.

Before I continue there's something I want to say. I've already mentioned my real affection for Stefano Bontate several times, but it would take a hundred pages to explain what kind of a man he was. When I was in Corleone I heard the Doctor say that only a saint, a mother and a man of honour were capable of acting disinterestedly. A mother always does, but only towards her own children. A saint always does, but only because he wants to be a saint and is hoping to impress the Almighty. A man of honour doesn't always act in this way, but when he does it is a gesture of friendship that asks for nothing in return. It is a hand held out.

That is what it means to be a man of honour, and Stefano was the last of them. After him there were only murderers and drug dealers. The Family he ran looked after me. It protected me, it taught me a great deal, it gave me financial security. My mother and father gave me their affection, they could do no more. My father taught me respect, but without power and without money there can be no respect, only dignity at the most. The *cavaliere* and the other people my father worked for did not respect him, yet he never humbled himself before them. Paolino and his brother did not respect his grey hairs when they beat him up, yet he died as a man, without informing on them. This is true dignity, and it was the most he could aspire to. Yet I, with a pistol in one pocket and money in the other, was able to command respect from all and sundry. Stefano alone, had he wanted to, could have made me eat dust. He never did. Nor did Cosentino or any of the Family friends.

That's what I wanted to say.

For two weeks I hid away like a mouse in its hole. I spent the daytime in hotels, a different one every day, or with a prostitute, making up for the monkish life I had led over the past two months at Mondello. The nights I spent filling my lungs with sea air.

At last Salvo assured me that everything was fine, and in fact he looked more relaxed.

'Next week we're going to Rome, Giovannino, and we'll have time to talk things over.'

Thus began a new life.

Nino Salvo was a different kind of employer from all the others. He was no *padrone*. He didn't know how to order people about, he allowed too much familiarity and asked too often for advice. He had been born with a silver spoon in his mouth and it showed. He was a wealthy, educated man and he knew how to treat people of his own class: politicians, beautiful women, top businessmen. He always knew exactly what to say and what to do. He taught me how to behave in society. He told me never to call anyone '*vossia*', sir, except him when we were alone if I felt like it. The title was old-fashioned and gave the wrong impression. 'We mustn't look out of place, Giovannino,' he said sometimes. 'And do away with these dark suits. Go and buy yourself flannels and a sports jacket, get yourself some pullovers and a cashmere roll–neck sweater.'

I had no idea about things like this, so to begin with he gave me his own cast–offs. Not that I couldn't afford to buy the stuff, but I didn't know how to go about it and I was afraid of making mistakes. He pointed me towards the right shops, telling me to use his name and not to be coy about asking advice from the manager or assistants. I now learnt of the existence of shoes at five hundred thousand lira a pair. This struck me as quite ridiculous! Not even Stefano, who was a millionaire several times over, would have dreamt of spending that amount on two shoes which would after all get dirty and wear out just as fast as the others. But he gave me two pairs for Christmas, and then when he saw me walking as if I was treading on eggs, he laughed and said I mustn't think about them or I'd never get used to such things. Don Nino knew how to live.

He had a boat, too. At least he called it a boat, but it was really a kind of ship, very classy and with every conceivable comfort. My trip on the fishing boat had seemed pretty special at the time, but when I found myself cruising off San Vito Lo Capo with the wind tugging at my hair and a cool drink in my hand, I was so overcome that tears came into my eyes. I was forty–six now and had lived in Palermo for twenty–two years, but at the end of the day I was still a poor, semi–literate country lad with mud on my boots, yet here was Don Nino taking me by the arm and saying:

'How about a whisky, Giovannino? Go on, help yourself.'

He took me to Villa Igiea,[1] where there was a marina for boats such as his. I had heard about it, but never imagined it would be so wonderful. In fact it had been frequented by princes and monarchs from all over the world, and the bar where he bought me drinks looked like a mediaeval church with its painted walls and vaulted stone ceiling. I was half expecting to be given a consecrated wafer instead of an aperitif.

And he taught me about travel. After three months I knew so much about advance booking, flight check–ins and foreign currency that I could have opened a travel agency. When he was teasing me once, he said I looked like an English lord, the kind that hunts foxes. I laughed.

'Hardly,' I said. 'I only have to open my mouth for everyone to realize I'm a Sicilian.'

'And isn't that as it should be?' he asked. He looked quite fierce. 'Is being Sicilian anything to be ashamed about?'

'Absolutely not.'

'Then let people hear your accent. Don't you dare try and hide it.'

Of course, he wasn't a man of honour in the way I understand it, but one can learn from everyone, whatever it is they have to teach, and in the short time we were together he taught me a lot.

He was not a brave man, either. He was afraid of his cousin, of the Customs and Excise and of the Corleonesi. Perhaps he was afraid of me too. He wasn't sure of his ground, he never felt secure. He spent hours and hours on the telephone at all hours of the day, and he was always having meetings with people: accountants, lawyers, business associates. Sometimes he would think he was being followed and I would have to check it out to put his mind at rest. Afterwards he would give me a present and stop worrying for a while.

But it was a worrying time. Every day someone died or disappeared. And when it was a person Don Nino had known, he would get the jitters. After Lo Presti it was the turn of Francesco Di Noto, then Don

Calogero Pizzuto who had helped me sort out the bank business in Agrigento. Don Nino knew him too. The day we heard of his death, he went round with a face as long as your arm: he looked positively ill. He had lived all his life surrounded by friends and allies who protected him. The friends were now more scared than he was and the allies were all dead. Only I remained to protect him.

It was either Christmas Day or Christmas Eve, I don't remember which, when they tried to kill *Scarpuzzedda*. He got away without a scratch. Three men died in the vendetta that followed immediately. Don Nino returned to Palermo a couple of days later. He had already heard the news. He took me by the arm.

'You see, Giovannino? The deaths are all on one side. The good Lord has finally decided which side He's on.'

It was about this very time that I ran into Saro *Menzapinna* in Via Duca della Verdura. I hardly recognized him. He was as thin as a lath and had grown a moustache. We embraced like brothers. He was so overcome, poor devil, that he couldn't speak for a time. Then he told me that he had escaped by a miracle when they shot Stefano's driver. He had gone into hiding at the home of a second cousin who had demanded an enormous sum of money saying that he was risking his life. And when the money was finished he chucked him out.

'Did you put a bullet through his head, Saro?' I asked in all seriousness. He smiled his usual crooked smile.

'Why should I risk my neck for a bum like that?'

I was happy to see him. I was used to being a loner, but it's nice to be with a friend now and then and have something different to talk about. We talked of all kinds of things. He told me about the friends who were now dead. Mariano had been killed before his very eyes, and his killers had bundled him into a car, a light–coloured BMW, and driven off. Only a few drops of blood had remained on the road and the incident hadn't even made *Ora*, usually more alert to this kind of thing than *Sicilia*.

Saro was running scared. I gave him some money, but what he really needed was a safe place to hide. All the old *pirtusi* had been blown; a few trusted contacts were all that remained. I took him to a shopkeeper in Via dell'Airone, a childless widower who lived on his own and had a large flat over the shop. He wasn't overjoyed at the prospect. Now that the Bontate family at Villagrazia had been wiped out and their enemies were calling the shots, everyone was scared. This was understandable. But he came round eventually, and for three months Saro was provided for.

'*U Signuri t'u renni,*'[2] he exclaimed as we said goodbye. I told him to be careful, not to go out alone for any reason whatsoever. The first free evening I had I would come to take him out for a decent meal. But although I didn't know it, Saro was already a dead man as I embraced him and tried to put heart into him. I never saw him again.

When I returned to the place and asked the shop-keeper to tell my friend I was there, he looked stunned and couldn't get a word out. He said he hadn't seen Saro since I had sent someone to pick him up.

'Who sent someone to pick him up?' I demanded, seizing him by the throat. But I knew what had happened before he told me. Two young men had driven up in a black BMW. They said they had come from me with an urgent message. And poor Saro had dashed out in the middle of shaving so as not to keep me waiting. The shopkeeper had suspected nothing. He was the only one who knew that my friend was there and only I could have sent for him.

There was a possibility that he himself had been the traitor, that he had sold us out. But I knew him too well: he might act out of cowardice, but never for money. Two possibilities remained: either they had seen us together by chance and searched the area for him; or they were watching me, and while watching me had seen him. And he was not under the protection of Don Nino; he was pig meat, my friend Saro *Menzapinna*, and his death would offend no one.

I never knew for sure what happened to him, but five or six months later I ran into a *picciotto* belonging to the Corso dei Mille Family. He told me in confidence that he had had no part in it, but he knew that Saro had been driven, blindfolded, to a certain place whose name he only told me in dialect and which I didn't understand. Much later, the papers carried stories, illustrated with photographs galore, about a death chamber at Porto Sant'Erasmo, behind Villa Giulia. On a wharf there, in an old building, Filippo Marchese and his confederates put people into barrels of acid. Nothing remained apart from the victim's wrist–watch and gold teeth, if any.

I don't know why they should have done this to Saro. Maybe as a favour to the Corleonesi, who wanted the entire Family wiped out. Or maybe Saro had been naïve enough to try to get in with the Corso dei Mille Family. And they had found a place for him, in a barrel of acid.

Notes

1. An old–established hotel near Palermo, built by the Florio family.
2. May God reward you.

XIX

In May 1982 General Dalla Chiesa arrived in Palermo. Don Nino took it very badly. As though the Customs and Excise, the Corleonesi, and the serious illness he had been suffering from lately were not enough to put the wind up him, now he had this to cope with, and I noticed that his fear of the General made the others pale by comparison.

'This will be the ruin of me,' he said. 'He's not messing around. Once he gets his sights on a man, he'll even want to find out the make of his razor blades. He's a Piedmontese *carabiniere* . . . '

He was expecting to be arrested from one moment to the next, but kept quiet about it because in Palermo he was thought of as highly as the Chancellor of the Exchequer. His cousin Ignazio, from what I could gather, felt safer. But Don Nino was worried, so worried that one day he did something I was certainly not expecting. He took me to a bank which must remain nameless, where he had one of those big strongboxes, and after I'd signed some papers he told me that I now held joint rights with him to that strongbox.

'I hope it's stuffed with money,' I joked as we went downstairs to the basement of the bank. But he wasn't in the mood for jokes. As soon as we were alone he opened the strongbox. It was full of papers; they must have weighed over five kilos. There were maps, receipts, photocopies of cheques, lists of names. Things that meant nothing to me. He explained that he was expecting a search and the papers would not be safe either at home or in his office.

'You keep the key. If anything should happen to me, get here as soon as you can with a big bag, fill it and get rid of it. Burn the lot. Understand?'

I understood, but I was most uneasy about it. There was always the danger that any investigation would lead to the bank and the empty strongbox. To get into the vault one had to sign a paper first. What would I say to the examining magistrate if I was questioned?

'You don't have to worry on that score, Giovannino. The manager here is one of us. At the first whiff of police activity, he'll wait until you've been and then make away with the strongbox and all signatures. Not even the smell of these papers will remain.'

I clipped the key on to my key ring with all the others and forgot about it. Nor did he mention it again after that day.

At the end of August, something happened that I had been expecting for some time. I had driven some guests who came from Rome to a restaurant, and was under orders to pick them up an hour and a half later. On my way out I met a member of the Family, one of those suspected of having sold out Stefano to the Corleonesi. He was with two elderly and elegantly dressed men. As soon as he saw me he stopped, excused himself to the others and guided me to a corner where he could speak without being overheard.

'So what, may I ask, are you doing?'

I would have liked to smear him all over the wall. In March, Totò Contorno had been arrested in Rome; all the other members of the Family were either dead or had vanished without trace; those who remained had turned traitor or slunk off with their tails between their legs. And here was that sonofabitch, fat and sleek, poncing in and out of restaurants without a care in the world. And he had the nerve to ask me what I was doing.

I told him I was trying to earn a living. He started to lecture me. It wasn't done, he said, to quit the Family like that. I had gone off without a word, without telling anyone which side I was on.

'The side of the living,' I told him flatly. They, of course, would have liked to see me on the other side, the same side as Stefano, Teresi, D'Agostino, Saro and fifty other poor sods. And his mention of loyalty made me laugh. He had always pretended not to know me. I'm certain he didn't even know my surname. At the time of the election he and others like him had prevented me from voting, and when business was being discussed my view counted for nothing or was considered last. And now *cumpari Minchia*[1] was complaining because I showed some lack of affection towards the Family. He was a Judas, a murderer and a man without honour.

The Family for me meant Stefano and possibly Cosentino as well, but for the rest I didn't give a shit. I told him as much, and his face went hard.

'You can thank Don Nino—'

'Don Nino and this,' I replied, patting the bulge over the pistol nestling against my chest. He said nothing, but as he went he threw me another black look. He was wasting time. A man like that could harm only those who trusted him. You simply had to take care never to turn your back on him.

General Dalla Chiesa was shot at the beginning of September. I heard the news on the radio. I always prefer radio to television: you don't have to look at it and you can get on with other things while you listen. It was late evening. I had my supper and went to bed. I

213

was thinking that in the days of Don Pepe Genco Russo and Don Calò Vizzini no one would have dreamed of shooting a high ranking policeman. But now here they were blasting away no less a figure than a general who was also Prefect of Palermo. And thinking nothing of it.

'They've pulled the big one now,' said Don Nino as soon as I got to his office. Knowing how anxious he was I took the liberty of asking if the news had pleased him.

'Not at all. It's serious. All hell is going to break loose now. I can already imagine the headlines in the press, the questions in parliament. It'll cause problems all round, you'll see. This isn't going to mean a let-up, quite the contrary! The men who had the gall to shoot the General are the kind who don't stop to think, who don't stop at anything. Do you understand my drift?'

I understood only too well. I had been stunned when they shot the Doctor. And when they had killed Di Cristina. And when they had blown off Stefano's head. Nothing could surprise me any longer. I looked at Don Nino thinking that maybe he, too, was destined to die with his shoes on. Those shoes worth five hundred thousand lira.

He got a ton of newspapers. I had never seen so many at any one time. They were all full of the shooting of Dalla Chiesa and every reporter tried to give the impression that he knew things that were not even known in Palermo. While he read the papers, every now and then Don Nino threw them down in disgust.

'Shit: what idiots they must be!' he cried, reaching for the phone and staying glued to it for hours.

There were hundreds of rumours but no hard facts. The truth is that the General's posting to Sicily was meant to show that the government was prepared to face up to its responsibilities. But they knew he had no chance in a

214

place like Palermo and that if he tried to do anything he would be killed. This didn't worry them at all: he could be impotent or dead, the choice was his.

'He was just strolling through the city like a tourist; no bodyguard, no armoured car, no gun!' Don Nino was saying on the phone. 'Who the hell did he think he was, the invisible man?'

But I could see he was breathing more easily. He made his calls with me in the room and didn't mind what I heard. Then one day someone told him his phone was going to be tapped. I was there. Don Nino's face fell. This meant that General or no General they were still taking an interest in him.

He changed telephones, using one belonging to a priest in the neighbourhood. The priest made sure the room was clean, brought him a cup of coffee and made himself scarce. I listened, keeping as quiet as a mouse and thinking. Don Nino made calls to Rome, speaking to big shots in parliament and the ministries. He had all their unlisted numbers in his book. These were the people who had warned him about his phone being tapped. Later they kept him informed about the progress of the inquiries, telling him who the examining magistrate was and what information he already had. Someone in the prosecutor's office rang him every two or three days and gave him a thorough rundown of the latest news. So he knew exactly what to guard himself against and was able to organize his affairs accordingly.

I thought about Marchese, Inzerillo, Cavataio: all those who had thought they were in control just because they had the fire–power. What price a Kalashnikov now! The telephone was the real Kalashnikov. And while Don Nino and others like him could put paid to any number of *Cavataios*, the men with machine–guns could only beg for favours. It occurred to me that there were some things that even Stefano had not understood.

The only people who could throw their weight around were the Corleonesi. They didn't look at the number of pips on the uniform before pulling the trigger. So, in the end, even Don Nino and his friends got frightened and tried to keep on the right side of them. I was there when he spoke to men who were on the run and knew that he met one of them one Saturday evening: I heard him fix the time and place and expected he would ask me to go with him. But in the event, I don't know why, I was not taken to the meeting and never knew the identity of the man concerned.

At one point the judicial inquiry started to pose a real danger. Don Nino was in a constant state of nerves and one evening, in his office, he let fly at the lawyer for failing to deal with the causes of his anxiety.

'They can get you for criminal association any time they like,' the lawyer was saying. He repeated it several times. And he was right, because the summons duly arrived and made a lot of copy for the journalists. This business about criminal association is something the authorities always trot out when they decide to arrest someone but haven't got a shred of evidence to go on. 'It's a charge that can include everything or bugger all, depending on the circumstances,' the Family lawyer had once explained to me.

The charge itself was unimportant. What mattered was that men as powerful as the Salvo cousins could be examined in this way, on their own home ground, by just any magistrate. Everyone said that it had to do with the tax offices, but according to a report I heard, they had got out of that business back in 1982 after an inquiry implicating some of the big noises in the region.

The following day I went with him to the villa next

door to the one where the Buscetta family had stayed over Christmas. He drove very slowly, talking at the same time. He said the magistrate had something on him and he didn't know what to do about it. He asked me if Stefano had ever found himself in a similar situation. I was surprised, because he and Stefano had been close friends and he should have known about things like this without having to ask me. Then I thought I saw the light.

'Don Nino,' I said, 'I have never shot a magistrate. Besides, it isn't something one could do alone. You would need the right weapons and the right *picciotti*, and for the moment the Corleonesi are the only ones in a position . . . '

I was about to add that, with all respect, I would refuse to lift a finger. I could take a liberty like that with him. But he didn't let me finish. He laughed.

'That wasn't what I meant, Giovannino. Who do you take me for, Al Capone?'

The subject was never raised again. It was the beginning of June. A few days later Captain D'Aleo was shot. Officers of the *carabiniari* had now become targets for regular shooting practice. So far Russo, Basile and D'Aleo had been shot, to say nothing of the General. It no longer surprised anybody. And it now became a massacre.

This didn't surprise me at all. Resigned to the fact that I might die at any time, I lived from day to day – but with my eyes open. I felt safe enough when I was with Don Nino, but when I was on my own I could never be too careful. I scrutinized the face of every man I met and looked behind me from time to time to see if I was being followed.

In the middle of July Don Nino told me to take a few days' holiday, to go back to the village. I really wanted to spend a few days by the sea at a little place

217

near Capo Zafferano, but he insisted on sending me to the village and I thought it would be a good opportunity to see how things were going there and do some repairs to the house. I had noticed signs of damp on the ceiling and wanted to do something about it before the winter set in.

I chose to avoid the motorway, which in certain cases can prove to be a death trap. Just short of Santa Caterina Villarmosa, I saw a 126 parked on the side of the road with a flat tyre, and a woman struggling to change the wheel. She flagged me down. There was no other car in sight and the surrounding countryside was good and open. I asked what had happened.

'I don't know how to change the wheel properly, and I've injured my hand.'

It was a nasty gash, right across the hand from the middle of the palm to the wrist. I bound it with my handkerchief, babbling nonsense in an effort to distract her. She was a schoolteacher, one of those spinsters who learn to get along quite happily without a husband. She must have been about forty–five, give or take. She couldn't possibly drive with her wounded hand, so I gave her a lift home in my car. She lived alone on the top floor of an old house where there were no other tenants.

She made some coffee and told me she came from Randazzo, that she was an orphan, and that her only relation was a sister who was headmistress of a school in or near Rome. Apart from her nose, she wasn't bad looking.

'If there's nothing else I can do for you I'll be getting along,' I said after a while, and when she tried to insist on my staying longer, I replied with the first thing that came into my head:

'If I stay too long, people are going to start imagining God knows what.'

'Who's going to start imagining things? The mice? There's no one else here. And I wasn't born here, so if people talk that's their look out.'

She was laughing. But I was not. I was looking at her and thinking. Maybe the time wasn't too far away when I would need a place to hole up in yet again, and where better than here?

'My name's Giovanni . . . '

I stayed for two days. I couldn't stay longer. *Signorina* Margherita was no longer a young girl but she had a young girl's appetite. Before I left she extracted a string of promises from me, but because I told her I was married with four children, she didn't ask for any address or telephone number.

'I'll call in again on my way back to Palermo.'

'And when will that be?'

'At the beginning of August,' I said, plucking a date out of the air. And that is what happened. In fact, only a few days later the examining magistrate who had been gunning for Don Nino died in Palermo.[2] So I imagined he must be back in his air-conditioned office, waiting for me to appear.

I left at once.

Notes

1. *Cumpari Minchia*: the prick.
2. This may have been Rocco Chinnici.

XX

I don't want to talk about my last months in Palermo. I knew something was going to happen and I was just waiting for it week in, week out. I stayed close to Don Nino and waited. I no longer needed to worry about his safety as I had realized they were not interested in killing him, at least not for the moment.

'We live a day at a time, Giovannino,' he said sometimes.

I watched him thoughtfully. He was an innocent, Don Nino, a man who had had it easy all his life. Used to a level path, the first uphill climb left him exhausted and discouraged. And he talked to relieve the tension. I can't remember all the things he said to me or that I heard him say on the phone. Filled with forebodings about the future, he complained about all the people who had received favours or money from him and his friends and told me about them: they amounted to half the population of Sicily.

When the summonses for the big trial were being issued at the beginning of October, I remembered these conversations. I perused the lists of the accused and wanted men. Don Nino had mentioned senators, regional administrators, industrialists and mayors, and a few judges and police officers besides. He never soiled his hands with lesser mortals. The ones I knew about personally were less grand: prison warders, postal service employees, doorkeepers, customs officers. But none of these, nor any of those named by Don Nino, has so far, to my knowledge, ever appeared in the dock. Only rank and file operators, with a sprinkling of doddery old men and dozens of wretched individuals who should never have been there in the first place. They put away a hundred or two hundred *pistole*;[1] at least these were silenced for good, but for every *pistola* taken out of circulation ten more sprang up ready for action. And every time one of the 'bosses' (as the journalists call them) was sent down for life, those waiting to take his place jumped for joy.

On All Souls' Day I went home to place flowers on the graves of my parents. Seeing that my relatives never thought about tending the little oil–lamp or occasionally cleaning the headstone, I paid the sacristan to do it. My cousin seized the chance to ask me what I wanted to do about the rent of the land as his lease was about to run out.

'We'll renew it, won't we?'

'I'm not sure, I'll have to think about it,' I replied. I wanted to say yes, but something – a premonition? – held me back.

In fact, even before I got back to Palermo, the Salvo cousins were arrested. The news exploded in Palermo like a bomb. It even made the television news. People could hardly believe their ears and I am certain that there were many fine gentlemen who were shaking in their shoes and ringing up their lawyers to ask: 'What do I say if I'm questioned, that I knew them or that I didn't know them?' I lost no time in getting round to the bank where Don Nino had taken me. The manager was waiting for me, looking as fresh as a daisy. He hadn't known who would get there first, me or the police, and if you ask me he didn't care. If I got there ahead of the police, fine, I would get the strongbox. If the police got there ahead of me, fine, they would get it. It made no odds.

I shovelled the papers into a plastic carrier bag, leaped into the car and drove off. I had no home any more, but lived in a pleasant one–room flat which Don Nino occasionally used for his own purposes. Naturally I kept a few personal things there, but no money, no papers and no pistol. Nothing else mattered, least of all the shoes costing five hundred thousand lire which Don Nino had insisted on giving me.

This time I took the autostrada. I couldn't take the risk of being stopped with those papers in my possession. I drove slowly to use up some time, stopping at a petrol station at midday to fill up the tank and eat a roll. The weather was fine, not even chilly.

I got to Santa Caterina just after the schools were out, the time of day when everyone is at home eating. I didn't know whether Margherita would be there or if she would be alone, but whatever happened I was going to hole up cosily for the winter while the dust settled, and had a contingency plan already worked out. In the event this proved unnecessary. The poor soul was so glad to see me that she burst into tears. I told her that I had flipped, that I had beaten up my wife, smashed the furniture, been sacked from my job and reported to the police.

'The *carabinieri* are probably out looking for me.'

She was all of a fluster; she didn't know what to do and could hardly believe that she had a man at her disposal, one who couldn't walk out from one moment to the next with a casual wave because if he put a foot outside the door he risked immediate arrest. That very evening we found a place under cover for the car. And, as it turned out, I spent the whole winter in that house.

During the morning, while Margherita was teaching, I went through the documents and tried to read them. After lunch I had a nap; in the evening I watched television and fell asleep again. In all my life I had never been really able to take it easy. As a child and a lad I had had to get up at four in the summer and five in the winter to work on the land. Later, even when there was nothing to do, there was always something on my mind – thank God – and even when I slept I always had to keep an ear cocked. After three months of eating and sleeping, being waited on and spoiled rotten, I felt like a new man, a boy again.

Sifting through all those documents I soon realized the extent of my ignorance. Reading a newspaper article is one thing, but reading those papers was a completely different kettle of fish. Some were handwritten and illegible; others had been written by lawyers in their own jargon; then there were notes and photocopies of cheques. It was a wild mixture.

At the end of two weeks I had read through the lot, but was more confused than when I started. Eventually things became a bit clearer. I burnt the less important items and went over the others yet again, one by one. They dealt with leases, with apartments given away as backhanders, with enormous sums of money that had entered Italy by one door and left it by another. This was big business, the world in which Don Nino had moved as a master.

Although most of the stuff was Greek to me, I could see that some of the papers were now useless because they contained details of contracts, passbooks and letters that by now, given that a good month had already elapsed, would certainly have gone the same way as the strongbox that I had rifled. I conjured up a picture of bank managers, regional officers and functionaries in a host of Palermo offices flushing incriminating papers down the toilet. They would have thrown out their own mothers to escape the threat of prison.

But the cheques were something else. The days were long gone when I kept money hidden at home. I understood all I needed to about banking. Here there were cheques drawn on banks in Rome or Milan, for example, cheques that had been endorsed many times over. Some things cannot be hidden. So eventually I kept these and burnt everything else. In the end even Margherita, who was as innocent as a babe in arms, noticed that I lit the fire every morning.

'But what is that you burn when I'm out, Giovannino?'

'Letters, dear heart.'

What else could I say? Letters from my wife, of course. Love letters. Margherita read teenage romantic fiction, the kind you find in cheap paperbacks on the bookstalls, and there was nothing about affairs of the heart that she did not know. She got all emotional when I spoke of these things, and asked me if I was still unhappy about the breakup of the family.

'A little, yes, dear heart.'

At the beginning of February I decided to return to Palermo. Margherita wept. She stroked my face and prayed to God that he would allow her to set eyes on me again before she died.

'Don't worry,' I said, but she, poor thing, had no way of knowing if I was being straight with her or not. And it was impossible to explain to her that I have never let anybody down and have never been guilty of ingratitude towards anyone who has helped me. Even now, whenever I can, I pop over to see her in the town where she teaches. It's a town by the sea.

When I reached Palermo I went straight to a lawyer I knew by sight. He was counsel for one of the defendants. I had found a cheque made out to him in Don Nino's strongbox. Only the one. I had the photocopy in my wallet.

'Please take a seat,' he said as I went in. The office was old–fashioned, its furniture dark like the stuff you find in church vestries. While I looked around me, his eyes never left me for a moment. He must have been good at sizing up people at first sight. People spoke well of him; he was an expert criminologist and charged high fees. And he was sharp, certainly sharper than me. But I hadn't come to put one over on him, only to say a few words. And I came straight to the point. Taking the photocopy of the cheque from my pocket I laid it on the desk.

'Perhaps this may be of use to you and your client . . . '

He looked at it and his face darkened.

'What does this mean?'

'You are in a position to know that better than me.'

He asked if I wanted money. I said no. He asked if I had been sent by someone. I said no. He couldn't believe that I wasn't asking for anything. He studied the cheque, thought, asked a question. And then he started all over again; he was like a hornet trying to get out of a room. Eventually he wanted to know who I was and how I had come by the cheque. Had he asked me that to begin with our business would have only taken two ticks.

I stepped out into one of those winter days that you only ever get in Palermo. It was past noon. I walked until six o'clock, looking at everything I could see. Perhaps I should never return, and I wanted to store it all away in my memory. When I was tired, I went back to where I had parked the car and headed towards the village.

As I drove, I thought about the lawyer. I should love to have been a fly on the wall, to have been able to hear what he was saying, to know whether he made one telephone call or ten. But one or ten, it didn't matter:

by now the information that I had that cheque in my possession would have reached the ears it was intended to reach. The effect might be nil, but then again it might give me better protection than an armoured car. My life might be over, or I might survive a while yet. But I wasn't afraid: Fate works in its own way and you can't argue with it.

As I drove I thought of all those who had fallen by the wayside: the corpses were piled high, and nearly all had met with a violent end. For the first week or so I kept dreaming that they were breaking the door down, entering the house and firing at me with machine-guns as they had tried to do in Corleone after making away with the Doctor. And I woke up bathed in sweat.

Then I stopped thinking about it.

Note

1. *Pistole*: pistols, i.e. gunmen.

XXI

Three years have passed since then. The only thing I can say about these three years is that I have returned to being a peasant. I work on the land, the land I bought and the land left me by my father. The other day the tractor turned up the tip of a plough-share that snapped off one September day when I was a small child. I remember my father sitting beside the mule, not saying a word, just looking at his hands. Too exhausted even to curse.

Village life has changed. One can live in peace, no one spies on you or gossips. In fact, Finuzza and I are often together and not even the cousin who lived next door and was so set on marrying her off knows about it. Thirty years ago it would have been all over the village in five minutes and the poor creature would have died of shame. Finuzza wanted a husband, but as Fate denied her a husband she decided to make do with a man.

Not that I've got anything against her as a wife: she's a good, honest woman who has had a raw deal out of life. But one can only make so many mistakes, and I made a mistake marrying Nuccia. A man is free to do as he likes, but not to involve parents, brothers, wives and children. This is a principle I have always tried to act on. But Nuccia learned about me eventually, from lips other than my own, and I am convinced that this is why she died. And had our son been born, either he, too, would have been killed or he would have spent a miserable childhood among aunts, neighbours and street companions.

Throughout these three years I have been careful to avoid becoming known. One evening, as I was returning to the village on foot, three youths who fancied themselves as bully–boys tried to get nasty with me. It wasn't robbery; robberies in these parts don't happen like that. At most you get a few individuals from a neighbouring village breaking into a bank or the post office. I knew that if I gave them a few ten–thousand–lira notes they would have left me alone quite happily.

'What's up, are you afraid?' they jeered, trying to push me to the ground. It would have been easy to lay one of them out cold and so teach the others their manners, but I told them politely that I had no money and no intention of reporting them, and when one of them seized my arm and tried to twist it, he got nowhere. The other two teased him, telling him that he had let his grandad get the better of him. And I, only fifty–three, but looking older than my years, laughed and did the real grandad bit, so the whole thing became a big joke and they went off like lambs.

On another occasion there was a quarrel about boundaries with the people who had bought the land next to mine and wanted to run a road half through my property and half through theirs. I also recall having words with a contractor who tried to overcharge me, and with a neighbour who had worked up north and come home minus his manners.

But I have never shed a drop of blood. The people who know me only know me by sight, and if greetings are to be exchanged mine is the first. I am only interested in the land. Nothing else. It's wonderful to work the land without the spectre of starvation leering at you, to sleep curled up under the sheet without having to keep an ear cocked for the sound of the rain, because sometimes rain can mean disaster for the crops, and at other times the lack of it can be equally disastrous. But I have provided against the drought with a good modern well drilled down to a depth of eighty metres, so the water is always there even when the good Lord chooses to withhold the rain. That is where money comes in useful.

It has other uses besides. I went to Switzerland for treatment for my ulcer, first to Bellinzona and then Zurich, being looked after by a doctor I got to know during my time with Don Nino, who actually died in Switzerland, God rest his soul. And it was money that made the treatment possible, because in Italy if you want to be sure of getting the best treatment you have to go abroad, and to go abroad you need money.

It's useful, too, when I feel homesick for the sea. When this happens I sneak off to Palermo without a word to anybody. I've bought myself a Fiat Strada, a diesel, a real beauty. I get there, book into a nice hotel, dine at a restaurant where the fish arrives all but alive on the plate and the waiters all wear black jackets, and then sleep with the sort of girl you'd never see in my village even on the cinema screen. Not for shoes, but for luxuries such as this my wallet is ever open. And when I've had enough I go home. Occasionally, someone sees me return and asks where I've been. I tell them that I've been to collect my pension, or to have a blood test for the ulcer, or to attend an agricultural fair – things any decent person can do.

I still sleep out in the fields sometimes in the summer. Not on the ground, however: I'm too old for that now. I've built a one–roomed cabin just to avoid getting wet if it rains. In the evening I cook a little meal and then go out and listen to all the night sounds until I feel sleepy.

'You've got everything a man could want, Giovan-nino,' says my cousin from time to time when we meet. It's not true. He has children while I don't. He has a wife while I don't. He never has to worry while I do. He's always asking me over on a Sunday, and sometimes I go. But I never lend him money. If word once got around that I could part with a few million lira without noticing it, that would be the end of my quiet life.

So I argue over a matter of five thousand and bargain in every shop. That way I keep a low profile, and sometimes it can be very amusing. Familiarity, however, is something I neither seek from others nor permit myself. Not out of arrogance, but out of habit. There was a time when I trusted everyone who belonged to any of the Families: and the Corleonesi came along, men who didn't give a snap of their fingers for the rules. Then I trusted only the members of my own Family, and traitors appeared who sent all the others to the knacker's yard. It's hardly likely that I would now trust a handful of peasants whose friendship is untried and who know nothing about the reality of my life.

My conversation is limited to brief exchanges about agriculture, crops and the weedkillers we're now using. And I don't have much time for talking anyway. Every morning I buy a copy of *Sicilia* and read it practically from beginning to end. Then, what with shopping, the odd job about the house and a cup of coffee at the bar, the few hours that are not spent working the land vanish in a moment. It's a simple life, but it suits me in my retirement. And I enjoy it.

Only two things from my past remain with me. Firstly, my pistol, always accompanied by a current licence. It too, however, is now in retirement, lying in a drawer of the commode. I never take it out with me. If my sense of security is misplaced and Fate is lying in wait for me round some dark corner, it won't make much difference whether I've got the pistol with me or not. I don't think about it and I'm not afraid. I intend to live peacefully and sleep soundly during the remaining years of my life.

The second thing preserved from the past is my store of memories. I have known great men, real men. And life has bestowed on me experiences withheld from most. Some of these experiences I have described, others I won't talk about. If a man has no secrets to keep, then his life has been empty and meaningless.

The best memories are the little ones, the ones that seem mere nothings in the telling. Certain summer evenings with my companions at Don Peppe's farm; the first time I drove a car and the first time someone called me by my surname and prefixed the *'signor'*. Above all, certain moments with my wife and my life in the Families for whom I worked. It must be similar for soldiers in wartime: they all know that they and their companions may die at any time and that, even if they survive, they will return to civilian life eventually and never see each other again. But in the meantime they are like brothers, because among soldiers all their needs and their thoughts are the same, so certain words, even if spoken in a whisper, ring out like bells on Easter Day.

And there have been those whom I have loved. Not only Stefano and Saro *Menzapinna*. And many whom I have respected. And many have taught me about life, that it is a wild beast, huge and ferocious. But even wild beasts nurse their young and lick their fur clean.

I have not been a good man, but I knew when I was doing something wrong. I have recounted only what I could recount, but my pistol has sung a last song more than ten times, not only for men who deserved to die but also for some who did not. This was something I put out of my mind while I did it, and even if I thought about it, I still went through with it for my own reasons. And one pays the price for having such reasons. I could fill a whole page and more with the names of men I knew who have paid with death or imprisonment.

I have been lucky. The life I led left me with only one scar on the leg and an ulcer. Everything else it has swept away: of my companions, a few have ended up in prison. They will never be freed. All the others have died violent deaths. I am alone. Alive and alone. My only companions are my work in the fields and my memories.

Memories, not regrets, however. Why should I have regrets? I could so easily have died in the mines like my brother, or I could have followed in my father's footsteps, working for a master, for a pittance, until the age of seventy; or I could have spent my life in a Turin factory making bolts, far from the open countryside, the sea and my parents. Is this a matter for regrets?

But I have lived the life I chose, the good parts and the bad parts as they came. And if I'm born again I want nothing more than to live it all over again exactly as before.

I have no regrets.

All Pan books are available at your local bookshop or newsagent, or can be ordered direct from the publisher. Indicate the number of copies required and fill in the form below.

Send to: **CS Department, Pan Books Ltd., P.O. Box 40, Basingstoke, Hants. RG21 2YT.**

or phone: 0256 469551 (Ansaphone), quoting title, author and Credit Card number.

Please enclose a remittance* to the value of the cover price plus: 60p for the first book plus 30p per copy for each additional book ordered to a maximum charge of £2.40 to cover postage and packing.

*Payment may be made in sterling by UK personal cheque, postal order, sterling draft or international money order, made payable to Pan Books Ltd.

Alternatively by Barclaycard/Access:

Card No.   ☐☐☐☐☐☐☐☐☐☐☐☐☐☐

Signature:

Applicable only in the UK and Republic of Ireland.

While every effort is made to keep prices low, it is sometimes necessary to increase prices at short notice. Pan Books reserve the right to show on covers and charge new retail prices which may differ from those advertised in the text or elsewhere.

NAME AND ADDRESS IN BLOCK LETTERS PLEASE:

....

Name ————————————————————————————

Address ————————————————————————————

————————————————————————————

————————————————————————————

————————————————————————————

3/87